IN JUDSON'S
FOOTSTEPS

A GIFT OF APPRECIATION
FROM
ABWE PLANNED GIVING
MINISTRIES

IN JUDSON'S FOOTSTEPS

NATIONAL CHRISTIAN WORKERS IN BURMA TODAY ARE THE RESULT OF THE WORK OF AMERICAN MISSIONARIES OF YESTERDAY.

Elsie Northrup Chaney

with

Jeannie Lockerbie

Association of Baptists for World Evangelism
P.O. Box 8585
Harrisburg, PA 17105–8585
(717) 774–7000
abwe@abwe.org

ABWE Canada
160 Adelaide St. South, Suite 205
London, Ontario N5Z 3L1
(519) 690–1009
office@abwecanada.org

 PUBLISHING®

Cover picture: The Golden Pagoda (Shwe Dagon)—
in Rangoon

IN JUDSON'S FOOTSTEPS
Copyright © 2001 by ABWE Publishing
Harrisburg, Pennsylvania 17105

Library of Congress Cataloging-in Publications Data

Chaney, Elsie Northrup, 1882–1972
Lockerbie, Jeannie, 1938–

In Judson's Footsteps
  Missions, Non-fiction
  ISBN 1-888796-25-1

Printed in the United States of America.

TABLE OF CONTENTS

Hill
Stations
Sinlumkaba
Bhamo

Tiddim

Chin Hills

MYANMAR
(BURMA)

Taunggyi

BAY OF

BENGAL

(RANGOON) Insein
YANGOON ⊛
Maubin
Moulmein

PROLOGUE

"This is Burma, and it will be quite unlike any land you know."

These words from Rudyard Kipling are still true today, more than 100 years after he wrote them. Today Burma is called *Myanmar,* and its capital, Rangoon, is known as *Yangon.* It is the largest country on mainland Southeast Asia, with an area of 676,000 square kilometers in a highly strategic location between India and China. Much of the country lies along the Bay of Bengal, part of the Indian Ocean. The population in 2001 was approximately 50 million and comprised of 135 different people groups. About 87% of the population is Buddhist, 7% is Muslim, and a sizable Christian presence exists among the minority groups.

(Adapted with permission from *Global Prayer Digest.*)

In 1990 George Collins, international director of GAP Ministries, and Jim Long, GAP representative for the Indian subcontinent, attended the 175th Anniversary Celebration of Adoniram Judson's arrival in Burma. Due to political unrest, the celebration could not be held exactly 175 years after Judson's 1813 arrival. Despite upheaval in the country, about 10,000 guests participated in the celebration. Only 10 of those guests were foreigners. George and Jim were two of them.

Jim writes his account of the event: "We were impressed that this special event was entirely planned by Burmese nationals. In fact, foreign missionaries have been absent from Burma since 1966, when they were forced to leave the predominantly Buddhist nation.

"Burmese Christians receive some outside funding for specific projects, but for the most part, national leaders make plans after asking the Lord for help, strength, and direction. They have learned to be independent.

"The icing on the cake was the music; songs of praise lifted up to the glory of God. The early missionaries are to be commended for following the apostle Paul's admonition in introducing the Burmese believers to the offering of praise in song. *'Speaking to yourselves in psalms and hymns and spiritual songs, singing and making melody in your heart to the Lord'* (Ephesians 5:19).

"We were saddened to meet descendants of Adoniram Judson's converts who are not living for the Lord. That is a good object lesson for us: our relationship with Christ must be personal. God has no grandchildren. Each generation has a great responsibility to make sure the next generation knows the way of salvation through repentance and faith in the Lord Jesus Christ.

"We also met brothers and sisters in Christ who are affiliated with the Evangelical Baptist Churches of Burma. This fellowship of nearly 100 churches among the Chin peoples of southeastern Burma has demonstrated faithfulness and commitment to Christ's cause through the years."

Who are these people who follow in Judson's footsteps?

TESTIMONIES OF NATIONAL
CHRISTIAN WORKERS

Dr. S. N. Mang, president, Faith Baptist Bible College
I was born on April 21, 1955, in Tiddim, Chin State, Burma.
I attended the Zomi Baptist Academy from kindergarten to
grade two. When the government closed down that school in
1964, I transferred to the state high school, then went to the
Mandalay University, majoring in chemistry.

Even though I had been a church-oriented person throughout my life, I was not truly saved until the age of 18, during a
revival meeting conducted by a local preacher. After my salvation, I began to study the Bible and discovered that man was
created just to please and serve his creator, God. This led me to
dedicate the rest of my life for the Lord's service.

Upon completion of my college study in 1976, I immediately went into the ministry as a part-time evangelist. Later, I
was appointed as a full-time worker of the Evangelical Baptist
Churches. During my ministry as an evangelist, hundreds of people were saved and many believers edified. However, the longer
I was in the ministry, the more apparent it became to me that I
needed further theological training. As I sought the Lord's will on
this important matter, He opened a door for me to study at what
was then called San Francisco Baptist Theological Seminary. I
went to the United States through India on an Indian passport,
and I earned an M.Div. in 1985.

Since I had been unable to find seminary training in Burma,
the Lord graciously fulfilled my vision and enabled me to start

Faith Baptist Bible College in 1986 upon my return from the United States. The college started with 50 students in a four-year program taught by four faculty members. By the grace of God, enrollment in Faith Baptist Bible College has risen every year. In 1993, we introduced the seminary program, a two-year seminary program for students who hold a bachelor's degree. Most of the seminary students are professionals: doctors, lawyers, judges, school principals, and engineers.

Faith Baptist Bible College has so far produced over 100 preachers who now serve the Lord in different parts of the country. And our students come from different parts of the country, representing many different tribes of Burma. This makes the school not just a theological training ground but also a strategic mission stronghold. But the college is not an end in itself; it is a means to saving souls and building churches. We need to enlarge our vision.

Recently, the Lord has given me a new burden for the local churches. I feel that, as a fellowship, the Evangelical Baptist Churches have fallen short of God's expectation of us. We could have reached more people and started more churches than we have. In the coming years, I plan to devote more of my time to church leadership. We need to launch out beyond our area, employing every scriptural method to carry out the Great Commission. I need the prayers and help of God's people now more than ever.

W

Rev. Do Suan Mang, professor and vice-principal, Faith Baptist Bible College

When Adoniram Judson arrived in Burma from the United States in 1813, he was the first American missionary to set foot in that country. He worked for seven years before seeing a single convert. Other American Baptist missionaries joined the effort to win Buddhist and animist Burmese to Christianity. Some of the missionaries reached the small town of Tiddim in the hill country of Burma's Chin State in the early 1900s. U Pan Za Kam, the descendant of a long line of warriors who fought foreign invaders, and Dan Lian Z Cing, daughter of one of the Chin State's greatest chiefs, were among the early Chin converts. In 1934, U Kam was one of four elders who built the first church building in Tiddim.

Five years later, U Kam and Dan Cing had a son, Lian Khan Mang. Lian Mang attended Sunday school conducted by the last Baptist missionary in the area, Mrs. T. O. Nelson. The young boy attended a mission school in Rangoon, 800 miles from home. Eventually he worked for the Burmese government. In the 1970s, Burma's socialist government arrested numerous individuals, including Lian Mang. During his time in prison the young man really studied the Bible, and accepted Christ as Savior.

A revival among Burmese Christians around this same time led to the development of the Evangelical Baptist Conference, and Lian Mang became its treasurer. Then, in the early 1990s, he joined Faith Baptist Bible College in Tiddim as a faculty member. He is now the school's vice president, as well as a church leader in Tiddim.

Rev. Do Suan Mang says, "I want to express my grateful thanks for the American people who brought the gospel to Burma."

***

Another Burmese man writes, "I was born to poor peasants in the Chin State of Burma in 1936. My father was one of four sons, three of whom served with the British Army. One of my uncles, a captain, was the first Christian in our village. Dr. Herbert Cope of the American Baptist Mission introduced Christianity to our area in 1910. He put the Chin language into writing, using Roman script, and wrote 26 textbooks in three Chin dialects. By 1941, a handful of people had accepted Christ as Savior.

"One of my uncles was married to a woman who was demon possessed, and traditional spirit worship could not heal her. She often tried to kill her husband, who had been discharged from the army as an invalid. Two strong men were needed to guard her day and night. We exhausted our family resources trying to cure her. At last my father, as head of the family, decided to turn to Christianity. I still remember the day a pastor and five Christian village elders came to our thatched house and prayed with their hands on my aunt's forehead as we children watched curiously. Suddenly, my aunt ran amok and all the men had to subdue her while the pastor continued to pray. Within two days, my aunt was well, and the entire family converted to Christianity.

"While attending the United Christian High School in Rangoon, I led the choir for Christian village youth. After two years of university, I joined the Burma Army until I was forced to resign because I was considered detrimental to the spread of Buddhism in the hill country. Over the years, I helped start churches in Burma and in the Naga Hills of India.

Today, true Christians in Burma often suffer for their faith. We Burmese Christians face a spiritual battle. But, to quote Sir Winston Churchill of the British, 'Give us the tools, and we will do the work.'"

Another resident of the Burmese hills recalls the contrast between his old way of life and Christianity. "My forefathers worshiped the spirits in water and trees; they sacrificed the blood of animals to appease these gods. By God's grace, an American missionary came to our area, wrote down our dialect, and opened schools. Through his ministry we saw the light of God not only spiritually but also in secular civilization. By 1954 the gospel reached my village, and my parents became Christians.

"As a child, I was a Christian in name only, not understanding what salvation was or why God sent His only begotten Son into the world. When an evangelist came to my village for seven days, my parents prayed earnestly for my salvation. Their prayers were answered when, on April 14, 1986, I accepted Jesus as my Savior. After my salvation, I could not keep quiet. I received a B.A. in biblical studies and began serving as a pastor. After three years, my church now has 580 members.

"As I look back on the story of Christianity in Burma, I thank God for the American Christians who came here, especially Adoniram Judson, who pioneered the missionary work in 1813."

And, finally, another testimony to the grace of God and faithful missionary witness. "The church I attend was started in 1884 by Mr. Ayn, one of Adoniram Judson's first converts. After a while, part of the group split off. My church continued to stand, winning people to the Lord.

"Mr. Ayn was succeeded as pastor by Dr. Ba Han, an educated man with prominent rank in the High Court. He emphasized the holiness of God to the exclusion of reaching out to people with the gospel. A great change took place when the present pastor arrived. He is zealous in evangelism. In 1986 the membership was between 50 and 60 people; ten years later, the attendance had soared to 800, with branch Sunday schools started in other locations. We also support evangelists working in the interior among tribal people."

W

Much of Burma's successful Christian witness today is a result of the Burmese converts spreading the gospel message throughout their country. But how did the Burmese come to know Christ? Myanmar (as Burma is now known) was forcibly converted to Buddhism during the 11th century. In addition to Buddhism, many tribal people espoused traditional spirit worship. So how did Christianity permeate Burmese society? Some of the story started in a little town in North America . . .

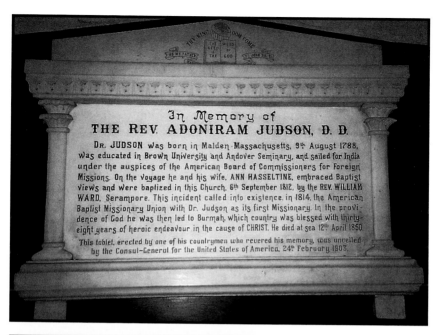

In Memory of

THE REV. ADONIRAM JUDSON, D. D.

DR. JUDSON was born in Malden·Massachusetts, 9th August 1788, was educated in Brown University and Andover Seminary, and sailed for India under the auspices of the American Board of Commissioners for Foreign Missions. On the voyage he and his wife, ANN HASSELTINE, embraced Baptist views and were baptized in this Church, 6th September 1812, by the REV. WILLIAM WARD, Serampore. This incident called into existence, in 1814, the American Baptist Missionary Union with Dr. Judson as its first Missionary. In the providence of God he was then led to Burmah, which country was blessed with thirty-eight years of heroic endeavour in the cause of CHRIST. He died at sea 12th April 1850.

This tablet, erected by one of his countrymen who revered his memory, was unveiled by the Consul-General for the United States of America, 24th February 1903.

Above:
Memorial to Adoniram Judson in
Carey Baptist Church, Calcutta

Above:
Buddhist monks

Left:
Pagodas

Vendors sell their wares

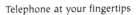
Telephone at your fingertips

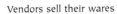

Street market

Above:
Modern Rangoon

Left:
Pagodas everywhere

PREFACE

To the Elsie Northrup Chaney Book

Although I never had the privilege of meeting my great aunt, Elsie Northrup Chaney, my father, Herbert Northrup, often told me of his aunt who was a missionary to Burma. As a young married couple, my husband and I received a Christmas gift from her, a copy of her delightful book *The Ivory Carver*.

Aunt Elsie's hand-written memoirs—a manuscript she called *To Be a Missionary*—were sent to my Aunt Grace in South Dakota at the time of Aunt Elsie's death. They were forwarded to my parents in Massachusetts with the understanding that my mother would transcribe the notes into typewritten format. Shortly after my mother undertook this task, she became ill with the cancer that ultimately took her life. The document lay dormant in my father's home for many years.

A few years later my father remarried, and it was my stepmother, Ruth Chase Northrup, who, after reading the pages written by Aunt Elsie, suggested the possibility of publication. I volunteered to take on the task my mother had begun many years before. As I read their story, I realized my Aunt Elsie and her husband, Clarence, were dedicated Christians, and I feel fortunate to have a part of telling their story.

My father's branch of the Northrup family extends from my sister and me on the East Coast to a cousin in Oregon and many others in between, particularly in South Dakota. I know that we in the family—and others unknown to us—will be inspired by reading about our aunt.

I am grateful to my stepmother, Ruth, for encouraging me to pursue this project. I also wish to express thanks to Pilgrim Place for furnishing pictures and information on the Chaneys at their final home in Claremont, California.

—*Susan Northrup Shaw*

Chapter 1

PLANTING THE SEED

My father's farm was one-third of the area in western New York State that his father, Grandfather Northrup, hewed out of the wilderness, twenty miles west of Rochester and seven miles from Lake Ontario.

Grandpa Northrup was born around 1806. At the age of 20, he moved from a small Dutch settlement on the Hudson River to Rochester, then a small horse-and-buggy town with stagecoach connections to smaller towns such as Penfield, Fairport, and Greece.

While working at the livery stables in Rochester, Grandpa Northrup became interested in land the government was offering in western New York. It was almost given away to anyone who would agree to clear and work the land. Grandfather had already acquired some property in the city of Rochester. He exchanged that property for farmland outside town. The hard work in clearing the virgin land meant felling trees and moving rocks. Eventually, the property was divided into three farms of 100 acres each that he gave to his three sons: Phillip, George, and my father, Francis Marion.

Around 1850, Grandfather Northrup built a beautiful red brick house, the first one in Monroe County. A hand-drawn sketch of "The Northrup Place" showed house and barns, and small outbuildings for pigs and chickens. I can only guess my grandfather got his dream of a palatial home from the early Dutch settlement of New York City.

The front door opened onto a long, elegant curved stairway

leading to four huge rooms on the second floor. Various closets were attached to these rooms, I was told, but I was never invited up to the second floor. On the ground floor, my siblings and I knew only the big hall with a parlor and Grandpa's room to the right. On the left of the parlor stood two smaller parlors, with the dining room and kitchen beyond. A big cellar, a big attic, and a covered verandah across the front of the house completed the structure.

Grandfather Northrup lived with Uncle George and his wife, Aunt Celia. Grandfather was a retired farmer, keeping very much to his own room where he had a desk, a swivel chair, and a small wood-burning stove. My mother sometimes sent us children to call on our grandfather. This was an adventure because the size of the house overwhelmed us. Grandpa always appeared neatly dressed in a white shirt and black bow tie. His white hair and sideburns gave him further distinction. Because he was deaf, we children did not linger long, but we loved the quiet warmth of his room, his kindly manner, and the pink and white lozenges he gave us when Aunt Celia led us out the front door.

Where Grandfather Northrup learned the art and skill of driving a six-horse team through mud and snow to carry mail and passengers, I do not know. But one of the family treasures was the old whip he used. The four-foot-long hard core of wood was bound with leather. From its base extended the snake-like pliable leather whip, probably 10 or 12 feet long, long enough to flick the lazy front horse. My father outfitted the big wagon with benches for Sunday school children and wielded the whip over a six-horse team at the annual Sunday school picnic at Lake Ontario Beach.

My family lived directly across the dirt road from Grandfather's house. My mother and father married at the ages of 21 and 22. The first of their seven children died from diphtheria and another child died as an infant. My family, as I knew it, included my big sister, Olive, my older brothers, Harry and Homer, and "the little girls," Elsie and Edith.

My childhood home was like many farm houses in New York State: two bedrooms on the ground floor in addition to the spacious kitchen-dining room, the heated living room, and the unheated parlor. In the long, narrow hallway upstairs, father hung a swing for us little girls. There was no heat in the three upstairs bedrooms other than an open register above the living room in Olive's room. At the top of the stairs a combined pantry-closet was cold enough to double as an icebox. From this was drawn—as needed—company desserts: pumpkin pies, fruitcakes, and other delights served on white damask linen in the kitchen-dining room.

There was ample space for Grandpa Brown's chair and couch, for he loved to settle in a corner of the kitchen. He was my mother's father, and blind, but we children loved to play with him, and sometimes played tricks on him, which pleased him greatly. On warm days we watched our two grandfathers sitting outside in the sun supplementing each other by their ears and eyes. Grandpa Northrup was a great reader, and occasionally brought his papers and good eyes to share with Grandpa Brown.

The only heat for the house in winter, other than the kitchen range, was the coal-burning upright stove in the living room. Here we spent winter evenings as a family. Sometimes Father played his violin and Homer an accordion, but the boys preferred their games. When tired of checkers, they pored over exciting stories in the *Youth's Companion,* and became so inspired with the wonders illustrated in *Popular Mechanics* that they spent many hours in the hayloft trying to build a flying machine. Their faith in that dream never faltered, though they never left the ground.

The village where we lived and other nearby villages in western New York were variations of the same name: Greece. There was Greece Center, South Greece, and our P.O., North Greece. Names for many towns, cities, and lakes in New York

State in the pre-1900s, were taken from Greek culture; for example, Troy, Utica, Syracuse, and Seneca. Greek was studied in every college, every theological seminary, and often in high school. No one explained these Greek names to me—nor would I have comprehended if they had—so I interpreted the name of my town as the "grease" I knew in a farmer's kitchen and tool shed. I was embarrassed when asked to name my birthplace to say "North Greece," wondering if I should explain or at least spell out the word lest people think "grease." But if I spelled it out, would I be thought an immigrant from Greece?

I was five years old at the birth of Edith, my younger sister, who became my life companion in spirit and affection. I remember my mother had not been feeling well that afternoon. The next morning when I learned of a new baby in our family, I asked no questions for I well knew how and when the baby had come: I had seen the doctor's black bag when he passed into Mother's bedroom the night before while the rest of us sat around the big coal-burning stove in the sitting room. For many years, I assumed that I, too, had been delivered in that same black bag by the same doctor five years earlier, on November 17, 1882.

When Edith was old enough to share my explorations, we enjoyed endless adventures in the chicken coop and the shed where corncobs were hoarded. These were used for quick fires in the house before the cruel cold of winter demanded heavy black coal to keep us warm day and night.

Edith was less than three years old and in my care when we suffered a serious mishap. The little creek which ran through our farm and looped near our house at one bend was a delight both summer and winter. But the spring thaws from areas beyond us emptied through our creek into Lake Ontario, seven miles north. When that happened, the low fields were submerged and the water was deep enough for my two big brothers to row a boat over the stubble of the previous harvest. They were always kind to us little sisters, and one evening Homer gave Edith and me a ride. The water was probably only three feet deep, but in the flood you could hardly tell where creek ended and field began. It was a delightful excursion until the baby fell overboard, struggling in the brown water and floating away from us.

The current traveled toward the rower. At my scream, Homer was alerted to grab Edith's clothing as she drifted past him. I remember her little round face as he pulled her out, fastened the boat to a fence post, and, with Edith in his arms dripping water all the way, restored her to our mother. I felt most penitent that I had not kept hold of her every minute. However, she had no memory of it and was not hurt—only frightened.

Homer and Harry were enough older than Edith and me that we did not grow up with them. We sisters loved and admired our big brothers, but there was no common ground of play between us. Girls did not play ball; they did not swim; they did not even play checkers—at least not with big boys.

Olive was older than the two boys, and to Edith and to me, she was another mother. She was artistic and handy with her needle, and as we grew older, she often made our clothes. Sewing—both by hand and treadle machine—was a prerequisite in any well-ordered home. Every girl had to learn to sew—at least my mother thought so—and I could not have been more than four when I began. By the time I was five, the daily requirement of stitching a square every day took precedence over any play hour, indoors or out. The daily task was to sew two halves of the one-inch squares of pretty scraps of colored prints. The next day, the two halves were sewn together to make a quilt block. This activity produced a bed quilt cover which my mother and a half-dozen friends quilted with delicate stitches in the winter hours. Sewn onto a colored lining and filled with cotton, the decorative, multi-colored squares produced a handsome warm quilt for my bed.

The country school I attended stood one mile from home, a pleasant walk even in the winter. But when the snow was too deep for short legs to wade through, my father gave us added winter joy by taking us and neighbor children on a flat-topped bobsled, which we often tumbled off (either by intent or accident), enjoying the fall into soft snow. If Edith and I were the only passengers, Father used the one-seated cutter, an open sleigh on runners (a true "one-horse open sleigh"). Bells on the harness made winter rides to school memorable.

I had the privilege of introducing Edith, at age five, to the little white school on the hill. At recess time, we girls ran around the schoolhouse. This was considered beneficial exercise as well as fun. After 15 minutes of continuous running, we reassembled in the one-room classroom and classes resumed in order, grades one through seven. Some classes consisted of one lone pupil struggling through grammar exercises. Others had five or more students, reciting the names of strange countries in geography class.

The last hour of each Friday afternoon was devoted to public speaking. Each pupil in turn must be ready to recite a short poem or declaim a famous speech of some patriot. Patrick Henry, Abraham Lincoln, and George Washington appeared before us in majesty. Even if a beginner said no more than a verse or two of "Mary Had A Little Lamb," the speaker was treated with respect. In a world where "children should be seen but not heard," this bit of publicity was radical, and some of the tax-paying farmers thought it a waste of time.

The joys and pleasures of growing up on a farm were simple, but never dull. The long, idle summer offered special treats. Edith and I had time to saunter up the long lane and find all sorts of surprises in the wood lot—a small spot of uncleared virgin forest set apart from the cultivated fields. The creek, never more than a brook in the summer, was a place of charm. Edith and I and our beloved pet, a water spaniel named Major, spent hours along its banks and under the cool bridge, finding such a variety of life in the creek and grasses beside it that we thought it as interesting as museums we saw years later.

The barn was another source of interest, especially the hay-mow on the upper floor. In the cold winter, the animals below added a touch of warmth, but not enough to heat the hayloft. When the weather was too severe for outdoor play, my sister and I had books to read and games to play indoors.

In the spacious kitchen and dining room, the table could be set for 12 or more. On weekdays the tablecloth was red-checked cotton, but on Sundays it was always white linen, washed and ironed in the same kitchen. I was proud when I was trusted to iron the long, white linen cloth. It had to be wet and ironed dry, at least dry enough so that as the folds dropped from the ironing board to newspapers on the floor, the cloth didn't get any new creases. The process involved changed the stove-heated flat irons or—a new invention of my era—the high box iron filled with red charcoal.

Sunday was a special day. Some children were allowed to sit in a swing on a Sunday, but not allowed to swing. Our Sunday observance was not as rigid as that; I was allowed to swing. Of course, only the most necessary chores were done. The stock must be fed, cows milked, and the work of cleaning milk pails and skimming cream done, but not churning milk into butter.

I remember once when my mother was painfully tempted to churn before church one Sunday morning to save a sizable lot of heavy cream which she said would not keep until Monday. I stood beside her in the cool, damp cellar as she pondered how far her Christian conscience permitted her to go in this critical situation. The butter and egg money was hers—both the earning and spending of it. Perhaps her decision to leave the cream and take the risk of losing valuable income was based on not want-ing to set a careless example for us children in the time-honored sanctity of the Lord's day. After long hesitation, she returned the heavy, unchurned cream to the shelf.

My father was no great help to her in this matter. He kept

the Sabbath as all farmers in our locality did, but he did not attend church often. Grandmother Northrup's maiden name was Wesley, but in what way our family related to that other English family of the same name, I never learned. My father had been raised Methodist, but during his youth in a boys' boarding school had been influenced by the anti-church, anti-Christian writings of Bob Ingersoll. Father separated from the Methodist church and married my mother, a Baptist. She was an ardent church-goer and an enthusiastic supporter of missions. We children were all brought up in the church, though attendance was influenced by the seasons, for we had a five-mile drive to the nearest Baptist church. I can still picture the great clumps of soft mud that dropped from the buggy wheels in spring and the clouds of dust we kicked up in summer. Church attendance in the winter was erratic since the snow was often too deep for travel.

Had my father continued in the Wesleyan tradition, we all would probably have been Methodists. Having inherited our Baptist connection through our mother and Grandfather Brown (who was Scottish), we blossomed into enthusiastic Baptists. I know I found abundant spiritual instruction and conviction of faith in Sunday school and church. The little Baptist church in Hilton had a two-keyboard pipe organ, played by the elegant wife of the owner of Hilton's biggest store. Two boys worked the air pump behind a screen at the back of the aspiring choir. When I heard the "Pilgrims Chorus" first sung on the stage of the Metropolitan Opera House in New York City, I knew the organ-ist in the Baptist Church in Hilton had prepared me well for this enjoyment.

We regarded the Bible without question as a holy book. The Old Testament was full of breathtaking stories my mother read to her children on Sunday afternoons. Edith and I found the New Testament not so entertaining beyond the Gospels. What we learned of Epistles and other New Testament books came from Sunday school and sermons. We always had memory verses to learn, and I have been thankful for that.

Nor did my mother neglect other avenues of culture for her daughters. Believing that every girl should have training that would make her self-supporting and independent, Olive was financed for a course in a business school in the city. She and a friend were given tuition for classes. They lived at a boarding house and came home on weekends. I was fascinated at the notebooks she showed me of peculiar marks—dashes, hooks, crooked lines—which she called shorthand and could translate into words. After one short term, Olive resettled happily at home, making clothes for herself, Edith, and me, and helping Mother with a new venture to bring income to the household. A line of the New York Central Railroad opened between Rochester and Watertown in upper New York. It would follow the line of Lake Ontario, and pass North Greece within a half mile of our house. The work gangs were all foreigners, mainly Italian, as I remember. They slept in cabooses on the siding and were fed by nearby neighbors. About 25 hungry men crowded our big kitchen every day at noon. They ate a hearty meal, and Mother, with Olive's help, reaped a good profit from the railroad.

Mother knew man (and woman) does not live by bread alone. She brought the blessing of music and art into our home. I had long begged for an organ. At church on Sunday no one better understood or listened more intently than I to every note played by the organist. At the end of our five-mile drive to church, I sat entranced by every note.

After Olive's short adventure in the city, my mother turned my older sister's fancy and ambition to painting. Olive responded wholeheartedly, working at an easel in the living room. The itinerant art teacher from Hilton stopped weekly on his round of country pupils. He was also a music teacher, and after weeks of my pleading for an organ and when Mother had a good surplus of butter and egg money, a high Estey organ took its place in our parlor. When the painting and music teacher made his rounds, I had lessons on the organ. Nothing discouraged me in learning how to keep the bellows full by foot power. I pulled out and pushed in whichever stops—at least to my mind—produced the enchanting variety of tone and sounds I heard on Sunday from the two-keyboard organ. This was pure joy. No one had to urge me to practice. The teacher supplied the necessary books (at cost price), and soon I was familiar with the best-known strains of the great composers.

These were hauntingly beautiful, but a new joy came when I learned the deep harmonies of hymns. I exploited these to the full when my teacher showed me the trick of holding deep bass notes while the soloist sang "Lead me gently home, Father" and the bass repeated the descending "Lead me gently home, Father." This hymn became my lifelong favorite.

My music was never of an exhibition grade. It was enjoyment to the ear—or so I thought. Along with playing the organ, I sang, and Homer, who had a good tenor voice, often sang with me, mostly simple songs of the day. The words mattered little if the harmony pleased the ear. Mother, a zealous white ribbon temperance advocate, seemed not disturbed that "Drink To Me Only With Thine Eyes (and I'll not ask for wine)" was our favorite. "Just A Song At Twilight" was another. On my own I could do "Oh, For the Days of the Kerry Dancers" in prima donna style. When freed of my daily work routine, I ran to the organ stool.

In the free hours of her day, Olive created what we all considered a magnificent painting of three heads of the frightened horses, called "Pharaoh's Horses." By this time, Olive had a regular beau who came often for long Sunday afternoons. George worked at a hospital in Rochester, though he was country born not far from Hilton. This painting of three horses' heads was George's special favorite, and we all admired Olive's work as it grew more and more to express the horror and fright of these animals who saw the flood waters of the Red Sea closing over them. God had avenged His chosen people, the Israelites, now safely on the other side, and here was God's unfailing judgment on the wicked king who had refused to "Let my people go."

A Christian mother and a Christian church taught me about God, and I responded to His call. I received Christ as my Savior and was baptized when I was 12 years old. This was a serious decision both for me and for my mother, who made it a special matter of prayer as she knelt beside my bed. The foreign mission enterprise of churches in the United States was gaining much attention at that time, and my mother was enthusiastic about it. The Baptists had more than a casual interest in missions for they (unwittingly) had placed on the shores of Asia, the first American missionary—Adoniram Judson, in Burma. The call was for every woman in the Baptist denomination to contribute one dollar a year to support missions. My mother carefully planned for that dollar, saving it in small coins when it could be spared from household necessities. To my mother's interest and encouragement of my music, she now added frequent mention of the deplorable spiritual and physical state of the "heathen," the name given to those who had never had the chance to know that God and salvation for man existed. They were more to be pitied than those around us who knew the truth but spurned it.

My mother marketed our farm's butter and eggs by selling the produce in the city 20 miles away. Traveling to the city was an all-day trip, and Mother often took me with her for company. We started in the early morning. I remember some of the beautiful homes and buildings we passed, especially the mysterious St. Bernard's Roman Catholic Monastery, built of stone. Golden one-pound pats of butter stamped by mother's ladle with roses on top and fresh eggs were sold to Mother's regular customers. With cash in her purse, she left the horse in a livery stable and we rode a horse-drawn trolley car to the big shops in town. I remember the materials Mother looked at, fingered, paused to reckon the cost, and often had to leave behind. There were many needs to be met at home, and she knew them all. To encourage me in my efforts at the organ, Mother usually took me to a music store and allowed me to select any piece of sheet music I wanted. On the way home, it was often hot and the trip seemed long. That was when Mother brought out *The Helping Hand,* a missionary magazine which I read aloud to her. The need for more missionaries was always stressed. I knew and wept about people on the other side of the world long before I knew about native Indians and blacks in my own land. I learned that India was a country where devoted, loving mothers threw their babies in front of the ponderous juggernaut car as a sacrifice to the gods, or threw them in the river as an offering to another god. Child marriage and its horrors, the young widows bound to the funeral pyres of husband or, if spared that, to become unwanted, oppressed outcasts for the rest of their lives, were horrors I related to my mother while we jogged along in clouds of dust. Later in life, I learned that these were not simply horror stories, but true facts of India at that time. Under the British Empire, such atrocities were prohibited by law, but I know of one case reported in the papers where a new widow insisted that joining her husband on the funeral pyre was her right. She evidently preferred an agonizing but short death to the alternative.

More than once during the long buggy rides, Mother turned my thoughts toward the challenge surging through churches for volunteers for foreign mission service. She asked me outright if I shouldn't consider joining. Around the same time, an outstanding young college graduate from our church went to Japan. Soon after that, the pastor of our church, W. L. Furgeson, announced his resignation and told the congregation he was going to India. He was a married man with a wife and two daughters. There was loud opposition to his taking a family to India, the loudest from townsfolk who were not part of the church or in any way affected by consideration for the people of India. One person said, "He might as well give those two little girls a dose of poison right now. None of them will ever come back." There was no sympathy for foreign mission outside the churches—and very little *inside* some churches.

But foreign missions had caught my interest and my sympathy even then. The more immediate aim of my life was to be a teacher. This, too, was my mother's hope as she made arrangements for me to enter high school in Hilton. In order to attend high school, I needed a bicycle for fair weather, a horse and buggy for rainy days, and, for winter, a home in town where I could live from Monday morning till late Friday afternoon. I had a shining two-wheeler with divided framework—a ladies' bicycle that could be mounted gracefully in long skirts. Pedaling over dirt roads was strenuous exercise, but I relished it.

In the winter, I lived with an elderly widow in a two-storied house. I actually learned much more from living in town than I learned in school. I soon had many new friends and was able to attend church suppers, young peoples' groups, and other meetings. The streets had gaslights. No more intense darkness, even outside! I loved watching the lamplighter carry his ladder from light to light, climb the ladder, open the glass lamp, and turn it into shining light—especially when that same boy wanted to walk me home from the Christian Endeavor meeting at church.

Buying books for school added extra expense, but a new avenue of income opened for children and adults who did not mind working in the hot summer sun. Farmers had found a new, quick crop for idle fields. Acres of red raspberry plants grew in long rows, waist high. When schools closed in June, the farmers were ready for pickers to harvest the thimble-sized, fragrant berries. From 7 a.m. till 5 p.m. for the six-week-long season, my classmate Ella stood on one side and I on the other, singing through the sunny hours. We received two cents for each quart basket we picked. Sun and rain did not allow steady daily work, but when conditions were right, we picked 50 baskets a day. We took a picnic lunch, supplementing it with as many berries as we wanted. We earned enough to pay the cost of schoolbooks, pencils, ink, and other incidentals for the year.

Chapter 2

NOURISHING THE DREAM

As the century neared its close, my home and family were shaken by the death of my mother in September 1899. Olive took care of Mother during her three-week illness. The Hilton physician diagnosed typhoid fever and prescribed some medicine he thought would help, but little was known about treatment of the disease

The pattern of our home was sadly broken. My elder brother, Harry, had already left New York State. He moved west to farm in a big way. He lived temporarily in Indiana, where he fell in love and married. Some years later the lure of big fields of wheat and corn took him to South Dakota.

Homer was now interested only in machinery and the impressive railroad engine, powered by steam, certain that farming of any kind was no life for him. Father, who had never been "sold" on farming himself, sympathized with the boys. He declared that he too would gladly leave the farm for an engine, and refused to dictate to his children as his father had done to him.

Another issue had to be considered. Olive and George had been engaged for seven years, waiting for the time when she could be spared from the work at home. By 1899, Olive's marriage was scheduled for the very month Mother died. All wedding plans were dropped while the farm, house, and equipment were sold at public auction. Father bought a house in Hilton; I was to finish my education and become a teacher as Mother planned. So Homer went to work at Manitore Beach while

Father, Olive, Edith, and I made a new home in Hilton. Olive would remain with us another year to get me started as the homemaker and housekeeper for Father and Edith. Another unexpected complication arose for her long-delayed marriage. This time I came down with typhoid fever. Being in town, I probably received better medical attention than my mother had, but I barely recovered when Homer, too, came down with typhoid. Olive, assisted by a practical nurse, looked after him. Finally, in the late summer of 1900, Olive and George Bennett were married in the front parlor of our Hilton house; I played Lohengrin's "Bridal Chorus" on the pedal organ.

In all this change I lost nearly a full year of school, so I was well into my teens when I finished high school. Then Father, Edith, and I moved to Brockport, where I entered State Teachers Training College. My secret plan was to become a missionary, but I never mentioned that to anyone. My job at that time clearly was to keep house for Father, although he thought only of looking after Edith and me. He could always find work as a carpenter, for he was handy with tools. He wanted no interests other than those that contributed to our happiness. Edith was in grade school, and if her free hours were spent in making friends in the neighborhood, I heard all about it on Saturday when she helped me with the week's laundry, baking, and cleaning. Our work was never irksome to either of us, and was often interrupted by gales of laughter. Father accompanied us to church on Sunday, but took no other part in our religious life.

My daily class work at the teachers' college lasted from 9 a.m. to 3 p.m. All preparation had to be done at home. That meant rising early to study, prepare breakfast and clean up, change clothes, and hurry to school. I tried to study in the evening as well, but I could never hold to that for long. It was more to my liking to rise at 4 a.m. than to prolong evening study till 11 p.m. Only once was I late for the 15-minute chapel service that began each day. That meant a personal appearance in the principal's office. To his question "Why were you late?" I truthfully stated, "Our clock at home was slow." He hesitated, his pencil poised above the attendance sheet, then said, "Well, that excuse is good for once!" and motioned me out. I was shocked and near tears that he doubted my word. In every home I knew, it was the father's responsibility to wind the family clock at bedtime. If my father had forgotten just one time, I could forgive him. Why could the principal not forgive me?

The principal did not know I would never willingly skip chapel, for I loved it. The program included two songs, Scripture reading (sometimes with comments), announcements, and the Lord's Prayer at the close. Mostly we sang hymns, but not always. Rudyard Kipling's warning to the British Empire—"Recessional"—had just been set to music. When we young Americans sang "Lord God of Hosts, be with us yet, Lest we forget, lest we forget," I sensed a new world of men and nations. I committed every word of the poem to heart. The words stayed with me all my life. When I became a participant of that final recessional of the British Empire in 1942 and saw the agony of local people trying to leave Burma ahead of the Japanese invasion, fleeing to the uncertain "safety" of India, I recalled the familiar words:

> *"For frantic boast and foolish word,*
> *Thy mercy on thy people, Lord.*
> *Lest we forget. Lest we forget."*

A broad education was the accepted standard of schools in that era, rather than the selective studies of today. Of course, the important part of my training was teaching in the Practice School on campus. We student teachers taught a few hours each day under supervision. At the same time, we studied a variety of subjects: geometry, physics, history, English, astronomy, chemistry, and others. Some I loved; some I hated—as indicated by my marks in the final examinations.

Brockport at that time had two sororities for girls and two

fraternities for boys. I had little time for social life and play, and was much surprised to be told I had been elected into membership of the Arethusa Society. To be an Arethusian gave a student standing in the school, something I never sought nor even desired. Only occasionally could I linger with the girls after school hours. Never did I participate in their occasional evening parties when fraternity members were permitted to attend.

Each year the public speaking class put on an oratorical contest. Members of the senior class were chosen by the English teacher to take part. A special original paper had to be written and accepted, then committed to memory. Then it was rehearsed with the speech teacher for declamation effects. The faculty chose judges from among the best-educated men in town. Even though the function was held in the afternoon, speakers had to appear in formal dress. I was one of the participants, and Olive made my floor-length white gown. The skirt was full with flounces, the underskirts likewise. The collar was high, the sleeves three-quarter length. The general effect was the popular "Gibson girl," even to the front dip of the waistline. The creation of this gown and the fine sewing proclaimed it as a wonder of sisterly pride and wholehearted love and interest, which Olive and George showered on me.

Townspeople rallied to this annual college affair. The position and poise of the speaker as well as the merits of the paper and delivery of the memorized speech were all elements in the final award. Miss Elsie Northrup was named the winner that year. I received a gold brooch the size of a silver dollar, with a wreath of laurel leaves surrounding the inscription. There was much rejoicing in the Arethusa room, but the surprise of a serenade outside our house at 8:30 p.m. by the fraternity took me quite off guard. What next? My world seemed full of surprises.

Having received my state teacher's certificate, I was ready to implement the first step of my cherished dream to become a missionary: begin teaching. That meant another move, this time to

Rochester with its many public schools. Edith was ready for high school now. Father could find work wherever we lived, and he found peace and joy as long as his daughters were content.

Father bought a little house near the new West Side High School where Edith enrolled. Although it was smaller than any other house we lived in, it had a roomy kitchen, dining room, and parlor on the first floor. A small but attractive entrance hall opened onto the stairway that led to three bedrooms above. In the basement, Father kept his workbench and tools, where he made many useful items. Edith and I became charter members of the new Calvary Baptist Church on Genesee Street.

Under the Rochester Board of Education my first assignment was to a first grade class at School No. 26, only two miles from our new home. With streetcar connections uncertain and badly timed, I usually walked. No. 26 was known as a difficult school in a Jewish section of the old city. The children were handsome and bright, but poor. Discipline was a problem. In those days, a class must be quiet during school hours. How else could they learn from the prescribed textbook in the teacher's hand? I was to teach them to write, read, and do sums. Primarily, I was to keep order by keeping them busy—and quiet—either at the blackboard (ten at a time) or at their desks. Such a dull routine. Poor little, eager students! Poor teacher who loved them and wooed them with tender words until one day one of the older, more experienced teachers said to me at lunch, "Miss Northrup, you can't control these children without raising your voice."

How could I shout at little Simon? I asked him, "Simon why can't you be a good boy?" He answered, "I'm as good as I kin be. I can't be any better than I kin be." I believed him and forgave him. I loved the children, the school, and the exhilarating daily walk. It was all another step on the path to becoming a missionary.

Then a Macedonian call to save a country school came to me through my mother's sister. The school was to be closed, and the few children to be sent to the town school at Holley, New York. But there was no system of busing. The proposal was a do-it-yourself plan. Parents were to deliver their children daily at the town school. Busy farmers would rather pay a teacher's salary themselves than be responsible for such a duty.

A qualified teacher was needed. The experience with a roomful of children—ages 7 to 15—at various grade levels was not a wasted effort. To organize, to control, to discipline, to keep all of them busy and interested was a challenge, both spiritually and mentally. I "saved the school," and counted it another step toward my goal.

Chapter 3

MEETING THE BOARD

After a few more years of teaching, I was ready to be a missionary. Edith was past 20 and competent to care for Father and a home. Olive and George, with their daughter, Mildred, lived in nearby Rochester. The way was now clear for me to follow what had been my mother's wish and my own fond hope. Yet the break with my home and pattern of living was not easy. It was an offering to God.

In today's world, where young people feel the urge to leave home, to travel, to see all and learn all, the hesitancy of my day to leave the security of the United States for a heathen land may not be understood. The only thing that made my leaving reasonable was my personal commitment to take up the challenge of the Great Commission.

The word "heathen" held no connotation of contempt, nor did it signify any level of inferiority. It was, among Christians at least, spoken in the spirit of compassion. It was the familiar biblical word used to denote those who had, through many generations of ignorance, worshiped substitutes for God. The system had hardened into the belief that the object itself was holy, even though it was a stone, a wooden image, or an alabaster Buddha. I had read stories of missionaries sacrificing their lives to take the gospel to the heathen. Now it was my turn to make sacrifices.

When I told my pastor's wife about my plans to become a missionary, she advised me to go at once to Buffalo, New York, where the officers of the American Baptist Woman's Foreign Mission Society were in session. Buffalo was only an hour away by train. Mrs. H. G. Safford, the Foreign Secretary of the Woman's Board, received me kindly. After hearing my story, she assured me that I was an answer to prayer. I had the very qualifications required for several educational institutions on the foreign field. I was introduced to the group, and interviewed by the gracious president, Mrs. Grant Edmunds, and others. Miss Agnes Whitehead, a soon-to-retire missionary from Burma, talked with me at length and asked me pointed questions.

Two foreign mission boards—both with head offices in Boston, Massachusetts—functioned under the Northern Baptist Convention: the American Woman's Baptist Foreign Mission Society appointed all single women; single men and couples were appointed by the General Foreign Mission Society. A requirement at the time for likely appointees of the Woman's Board was a preliminary year of study at Newton Center, near Boston. The Board would keep in touch with me and send further instructions after my case had been discussed.

I returned home from that day in Buffalo to a family council. I told them my plans to step out of the home circle, to leave behind those dear in my life, to go to some foreign land—wherever I was sent—to stay there for terms of five to seven years between furloughs, and to live or die there, as God would lead. It would be my all, my little, to add my life to the full cycle of the mission of the church in giving the gospel to those who had never heard it. All of this, of course, with the supposition that at the end of a year the Board counted me worthy to represent the living Christ in a heathen land.

Edith and Olive accepted my decision with pain, I am sure, but there was a touch of pride as well, for they, too, had been nurtured in the mission outreach of the church and knew our mother's devotion to it. George, who was an only child and had not been in close touch with any mission project, was troubled. He fully shared Olive's concern for Edith and me. He had encouraged all our ambitions. But this? He asked, "Are you sure, Elsie, you know what this entails?"

Father remained silent. The whole idea was outside his world, but in a private conversation he assured me of his consent. He did so, not because of his interest in the heathen, but because his own father had demanded that his three sons become farmers. My father hated farming, and above all else wanted a chance to run the fascinating new steam engines that tore through the little hamlets at 25 miles an hour with a whistle that called his heart. He said he vowed long ago that he would never deny his children the right of personal choice in any honorable work they wished to do.

Both my brothers supported my decision. They were faithful Christians serving in their local churches. As far as my family was concerned, I was free to go. The Board invited me to a year of study in Newton Center, and in September I took the train to Boston.

The year at Hasseltine House in Newton Center was my first experience of living away from home. Of the ten young women, all potential appointees to foreign service under the Baptist Woman's Board, only one—Esther Nairn—was from my own city. We attended classes in the Theological Seminary. We received good training, and I needed the courses we studied. But obviously the year of study served double duty, for the women of the Board lived nearby. We were entertained in their homes, where they could observe us.

The housemother could study us even more closely. Our dispositions, talents, eccentricities, dedication, and our capabilities were all under scrutiny and, without doubt, reported to and discussed by the women of the Board. We were well aware that we were being screened, but we did not resent it. We would have fared worse had the brawny, dour Scottish cook been the one to evaluate us. One Sunday afternoon, we were grouped at the piano laughing hilariously. The cook went to our housemother to protest. Such merriment on the holy Sabbath was shocking.

"And they are going to preach the gospel to the heathen? What sort of an example of Christian living is that?"

We lived in a beautiful three-storied, old-fashioned house. Each of us had her own room. From the flat top of the third floor, in the spring of 1910, we saw Halley's Comet in its glory—the great luminous tail behind the star covering two-thirds of the heavens.

I experienced my first ride in a car when Mrs. Edmunds, American Woman's Baptist Mission Board president, sent her driver to take four of us to her house for dinner. A great joy of that year was a week's visit from Edith, who, like me, had never been in New England before. I wanted her to share my experiences as much as possible: to sit in class with me and see the sights of Boston.

Ella Draper, one of our ten, invited me to her home in Worcester, Massachusetts, for Thanksgiving weekend. I experienced the breakfast pie still in vogue then, and other New England specialties. However, the glory of the Thanksgiving dinner was not the more-or-less common foods of that day, but the once-a-year special Thanksgiving pudding: a moist pudding made of yellow cornmeal. It was delicately spiced, rich in cream, baked slowly for four hours, and served hot with thick cream. As a result of that visit, the Woman's Missionary Society of Worcester adopted me as their special missionary and continued their letters, gifts, and interest in my life for many years.

As part of our training, we ten single women were given practical work assignments. Mine was teaching a Sunday school class in a town two miles away, a pleasant Sunday walk. At that church I learned not everyone in New England was highly literate. When the Sunday school superintendent read aloud the lesson for the day and said that Paul was bitten by a *vapor* (Acts 38:3), I was the only one in the room who seemed disturbed by the mistake.

Another assignment involved staying for a weekend in a

home for rescued girls. A social worker in Boston introduced me to the traffic by sitting with me for an hour in a notorious hotel. There we observed the number of male customers coming and going. As part of the weekend, I had to take eight girls to church. I was warned that one, named Della, needed special guarding lest she escape. This was a new and unsavory world to me, yet many years later I found myself working with girls in similar circumstances in Rangoon. I could look back and count this experience as another step on my way to being a missionary. I must have exhibited poise and a mature attitude, for as we left the church and I tallied the count, I heard Della mutter, "Oh, there's no getting away."

The end of the year was drawing near. One by one, each of us had to attend a Board meeting and be examined on our commitment. Did we understand that an assignment to foreign service meant for life? Would we accept the terms of the contract?

Examinations included a medical check-up. I casually mentioned the only flaw in my body was a small goiter I had had all my adult life. It had never bothered any doctor or me. Mrs. Edmunds' daughter, Violet, had a goiter, however, and the family had a horror of the word. Mrs. Edmunds was ready to dismiss me. Violet's goiter had given her family years of concern and great expense. "Oh, we can't take the risk of a goiter," was the Board's consensus. My missionary career might have ended abruptly right there had it not been for a missionary woman on furlough who happened to attend that Board meeting. She spoke up. "But ladies, have I not served you well for over 20 years? And I have always had a small goiter under my collar. It has never troubled me." Her remarks turned the tide. They would take the risk. I carried my small goiter under my high collars for years. It never gave me any trouble, and disappeared during menopause.

The next event of 1910 was the presentation of all appointees of both the Woman's and the General Boards before the Mission Board Committee. This was the company of new recruits being sent to China, India, Burma, Africa, and other fields. It was an impressive service. Some of the newly appointed missionaries were asked to speak. So sincere was their tone of commitment, it produced lasting links with many home churches.

After a farewell message, we ten women appointees separated to go home for the summer to prepare to sail in the fall. One of the group was asked by the Board to wait another year. One married and later went with her husband to India. My friend, Esther Nairn, went to China—and died there.

My summer was full of anticipation and preparation. "Take what you will need for six years," was the general advice given, along with an allowance for necessary purchases. In August, I received a letter telling me to meet in Boston for sailing instructions a week before the estimated sailing date of September 21. I was assigned to Burma, the exact location to be decided by the Reference Committee of the Burma Mission after my arrival.

None of the appointees knew much about Burma other than that the famous Adoniram Judson began his scholarly evangelistic work there for the almost unknown (at that time) Baptist Churches of New England.

Each member of my family was involved in my last summer at home. Father was concerned I might not have proper food. "We must feed Elsie well this summer," he said, and bought delicacies we could not afford. Olive was concerned about my wardrobe and sewed for a hot climate. High collars, wired behind the ears, were still worn in public; open necks were tolerated only on blouses worn at home. Edith delighted us all by her interest in every aspect of the preparations. She made delicious candy at all hours and kept the summer lively with her piano music. Like my father, who played the violin entirely by ear, Edith needed no notes. Whether it was a popular song or one of the classics, her fingers hesitated for a minute, then she was off in full harmony. That summer, at our urging, she began playing our father's violin. She had a German teacher who held her rigidly to the notes. She obeyed, but proclaimed it a slow way to produce music!

Our friends were mostly from church, for I had been active in various church activities. The young boys' club, the Christian Endeavor, the choir, and the Woman's Missionary Circles all claimed a special relationship. I knew their prayers would follow and support me. Occasionally I allowed myself to wonder if I really was prepared for whatever lay ahead. I had read that the Judsons at one time survived by eating rats. Would I have to do that? Could I do it?

Perhaps it was natural that taking care of my body was uppermost in my mind at that time. Those thoughts were justified on the grounds of health. Contracting tropical diseases was a probability to guard against. It took years for me to learn there are more serious things to guard against. Any leanness of spirit, or failure of patience, love, and understanding could betray the Christian way of life and the commitment which placed us in a heathen land. An incident of that summer introduced me to the price some pay to be a missionary.

Laura, a college friend, lived in Irondequoit, a suburb of Rochester. When I told her I was going to Burma, she mentioned a young man who, while studying at the Rochester Baptist Divinity School, had served their community as a student pastor. He was so well liked that when they heard of his plan to be a missionary, they made all kinds of tempting offers to hold him. But he refused. He graduated, married, and went to the delta town of Maubin, on the Irrawaddy River in Burma. Word had just arrived that his wife died, leaving a two-week-old son. The young man was advised to come home with the baby, but decided to remain at his station. His name was Clarence Chaney. I knew mission history was full of such tragedies. Husbands and wives laid their spouses and babies in foreign soil, and turned their lonely lives to the work they had been sent to do. Perhaps sometime I would meet this man and give him Laura's greetings and the news that the Irondequoit church kept its door open to him if he wished to return.

My trunks were packed and ready, the big, square brown one labeled "Not to be opened en route." That steamer trunk was capacious, to state it mildly. The tray of the trunk was filled with delicate materials, and a special compartment held hats for different occasions. Of course, we must wear pith helmets in the sun, but there might be occasions when social customs of the West (meaning British) demanded formal dress. For wherever the British went, they talked, looked, and acted British. We Americans were tolerated in their environment, sometimes even liked.

Our goodbyes were said—to Edith in private, where we prayed together. From that moment I counted Edith as a partner in my career. Her interest and enthusiasm for my work never lagged. Father came near to tears, but comforted himself by reiterating his unshaken conviction that he approved of my going, since this is what I wanted to do. Even then I doubted if he fully understood that I was under the compulsion of a higher standard than my personal choice. Olive, George, and Mildred, now 10 years old, met me at the train station, where I took the night train to Boston. It had been decided that one of the family must be present when I sailed. Since Homer, my engineer brother, had a railroad pass, he and his wife, June, would appear at the designated time of departure from the port of Boston.

Within a few days all the new recruits gathered in the offices of the two Baptist Mission Boards for the week of final instructions. Free afternoons were spent sightseeing and doing last minute shopping to be sure; for instance, buying enough shoes to last for six years.

Special sessions were held for the combined India and Burma groups, since we would live in a colonial government of the British Empire. Few, if any, had ever traveled outside the

United States. We would live and work under the protection, security, and hospitality of the British government. Some would go into evangelistic work, where long weeks of touring would take the men—and some of the women—into jungle areas. Plain wooden houses, called *dak bungalows,* were built and maintained by the government for civil servants. By courtesy of the government, they were available to missionaries as well. We could not assume that preaching the Christian gospel to the natives would always meet with encouragement or understanding from the local British officials, but missionary work was tolerated because it added to the ease of governing the local people.

If a missionary was put in charge of a school, as many—both men and women—were, he or she would find the government helpful, deeply interested in the literacy and education of the people. Government funds would be made available, well-established curriculums set, and regular visits of school inspectors could be expected.

In school administration or other field problems, confrontation, either by letter or in person, with these British officials could occur. We should be prepared for the differences in customs, speech, manners, and courtesy. We should know the acceptable ways of addressing people, for every approach had its long-established etiquette. We were told what to expect and advised to conform. Special occasions might include invitations to dinner or to the governor's garden party. We were instructed in the manner of eating and were trained to raise the food to the mouth with fork held in the left hand. We learned that a typical British dinner had a separate fish course with its own special "fish knives."

We were assured the British government stood ready to protect and act in all emergencies. We learned that all government letters were signed:

> *"I have the honour to be, Sir (or Madame),*
> *Your most obedient servant." (name)*

If a government official called himself "your most obedient servant," we missionaries could do no less, though this was a difficult concession for some Americans to make.

The general aims and purposes of foreign mission enterprise were reviewed, and the honor and history of early missionary efforts recounted. The established church in Europe had weathered flurries of dissent made by courageous individuals such as Savanarola, John Huss, Wycliffe, Tyndale, Erasmus, and others. Then the full storm broke under the leadership of Martin Luther, and the Reformation flourished, aided by the printing of the King James Bible in 1611. But not until the 1700s did the Protestant church awake to the final command of Christ given so clearly in Mark 16:15 and Matthew 28:18, 19.

Although the nonconformist church had been blissfully content to appropriate the blessings of salvation by faith rather than by works and sacraments, it was not inclined to share such comfort to the little-known and unappealing "heathen." Like most reforms, a single dedicated individual spearheaded the missionary movement: an educated shoemaker named William Carey. He boldly presented the matter of sending missionaries to preach the gospel. He told his local Baptist church in England that he was ready to take the Good News to India if they would help and support him. This proposition was lightly turned aside by a respected, elderly deacon who said, "Sit down, young man. When the Lord wants the heathen converted, He will do it without your help or mine." But in 1796, William Carey, missionary, translator, linguist, scholar, and scientist, arrived in Serampore, a colony of Denmark in India, east of Calcutta. Thus, the Age of Protestant Missions began.

The British East India Trading Company, fearing that missionaries would make the natives less easy to work with, refused passage on their ships to missionaries. Ships of other nations, however, often docked in Boston, New York, and Philadelphia, and in a kindly Samaritan spirit carried Christians from the newly independent United States to the "front lines" of missionary enterprise in the East.

Soon the spirit of love and compassion and the compelling urgency to fulfill Christ's last command stirred the hearts of American youth. Has not the youth of every age needed a cause—something worthy to which it will offer life and death? Here it was: a logical challenge to Christian obedience.

Seven young college men in New England volunteered for missionary service overseas. There was, as yet, no organized mission board to send them or to support them. There was, however, enough sympathy and understanding with their objective that in a church meeting they all were commissioned for missionary service. Six of the group of seven sailed. A year later, the last of the seven, Adoniram Judson, and his wife, Ann Hasseltine Judson, arrived in Moulmein, Burma, in July 1813. The Age of American Baptist Missions had begun. Adoniram Judson, preacher, translator, scholar, linguist, missionary, had become a Baptist while studying the Bible on-board ship. The Judsons were baptized in Carey Baptist Church in Calcutta.

The Baptist churches, having their first missionary on the field before they had ever heard of him, rallied slowly to the distant unknown land and their representative there. By the time I was born, in 1882, foreign missions had become a great enthusiasm of most Baptist churches, where the appeal for support was constantly and gladly presented in all departments. In Sunday school, children brought their pennies for "the little children of the world who never heard of a loving heavenly Father." Every woman of the church was asked to give one dollar a year for a special offering.

Better than monetary support was the offering of youth to overseas service. The well-organized Student Volunteer Movement (SVM) in the early 1900s sent thousands of young men and women from colleges and seminaries to China, India, Africa, Burma, and the South Sea Islands. Each denomination had its mission board, by which qualifications, service, and salary were regulated. The call to preach, educate, evangelize, and build the Kingdom of God on Earth rallied around the objective to "evangelize the world in this generation." This challenge swept through the colleges and seminaries like a Pentecostal breeze. Cooperating churches received furloughing missionaries with open arms. In fervent thanks to God, the missionaries shared triumphs of native Christians being saved and native churches being established in foreign lands, and appealed for the great unreached areas still waiting to hear the gospel.

I was not part of the SVM for it did not touch the training college in Brockport. However, I had been well instructed on the need for missionary work abroad. I read avidly all the missionary literature that came to our home. When I heard my mother planning weeks ahead for the missionary collection, I knew this was a special, serious part of her life. I had also seen the dedication to the call of overseas service when the pastor of our Hilton church resigned to take his wife and two little girls to India. When the only son of my beloved Sunday school teacher left to be a missionary in Japan, I hoped that I would also join the missionary record of that little town church. In fact, I was the third missionary sent from the Baptist church in Hilton.

Chapter 4

SAILING TO BURMA

The annual sailing of the new missionaries took place each autumn in Boston. An impressive farewell service was held at the end of the pier of embarkation. It was a religious service with officers of both Boards, members of nearby churches, and friends and families of the missionaries in attendance. There were short speeches, prayers, and tears—mostly in the eyes of those left behind. We were a fairly large group, for the new recruits going to India and Burma traveled on the same ship to England. My brother, Homer, and his wife, June, stood beside me. To my great surprise and delight, a hurried latecomer was Dr. Furgeson, just landed from South India. Hearing that Elsie Northrup, whom he had baptized in the Hilton church, was sailing as a missionary to Burma, he hastened to see me. He was now on his third furlough, and as he held my hand he said, "Elsie, I have only one thing to say to you: have patience! Have patience!" I often remembered that. As the years passed I realized that no message was more needed for someone like me who hoped to be "a workman not ashamed." After a few inspiring remarks and a moving prayer, we boarded the ship waiting at the pier.

Luggage had already been stowed on-board. Trunks sat in our cabins, and much more in mine: baskets of fruit, boxes of candy, flowers, and a mysterious parcel from Edith containing little gifts, numbered and dated one a day for the entire voyage. How and when had she been able to do all that? Now it was my turn for tears.

Why the United States shipped cattle to England I do not know, but for many years each missionary party for the East crossed the Atlantic on the Leyden Line cattle ships. Missionaries and cattle had little contact. Unless the sea wind hovered over the open hatch, where we could see and smell them, the cattle did not bother us.

Boston to Liverpool was a ten days' sail across the Atlantic. On-board were several single missionaries like me, but only one other from the Hasseltine House family of ten. She was going to India. On the next leg of the voyage, I would have ample time and opportunity to get acquainted with the missionaries going to Burma whom I had barely met during our week of instruction.

While we were engaged in the newness of our sailing that day, the city of Boston was highly excited about a different type of travel. That very morning was scheduled a demonstration of the wonder of the age: an airplane was to fly from the Boston Common two miles out to the Boston Light. Over water. With no land to catch the plane if it fell. How daring! We crowded the rail, letting the settling of our cabins wait, hoping to see this wonder. Somehow the timing of the airplane and the sailing of our ship did not meet. We passed the Boston Light and put out to sea, disappointed that we missed witnessing that miracle.

Ten days of sailing passed quickly, in spite of my spending two days in bed because of seasickness. On the third day, when the rough sea smoothed a bit, the steward persuaded me to go up on deck for "good sea air." I found myself wrapped in coat and muffler, steamer rug, and cap, stretched out in a deck chair, so weak and lifeless that my nearby companions laughed. But the steward was right; the "good sea air" worked.

The representative for the Baptist Boards in England had an office in London. He was the receiving and sending committee, the treasurer, and the business manager. He met us on arrival with a list of names in hand and began dividing the India- and Burma-bound missionaries by separating the luggage. We were taken to different rooming houses but ate our first meal together: boiled potatoes, boiled cabbage, and roast beef.

After a short wait, the missionaries to India sailed on a different line than those of us going to Burma would take ten days later. The Burma-bound group had opportunity for last minute shopping, last letters home (still only 10 days in transit), and sightseeing. Warwick Castle, Stratford-on-Avon, Buckingham Palace, St. Paul's Cathedral, and Picadilly Circus were not entirely new to me. Edith and I, for years, had invested our "all-day-sucker" money in Perry pictures at two cents each, purchasing 10″ x 12″ prints of famous European architecture. At the Tower of London, we saw a replica of the crown, which they told us was being cleaned and prepared for the coronation of King George V. The new king followed Edward VII, who, after waiting his entire life to ascend the throne, reigned only 10 years. Impatient for that honor, he had been heard to refer to Queen Victoria as "my eternal mother."

Missionaries to Burma usually traveled on the Henderson Line from Liverpool to Rangoon. The ships were named for cities and rivers in Burma: *Ava, Bhamo,* and ours, the *Chindwin.* The vessels made only one stop in the 30-day voyage, at Port Said. The ships were one-class passenger service whether your cabin was on the upper deck or below. My cabin on that first trip was on the lower deck. The mission representative proudly called the *Chindwin* "a brand new ship." It was indeed handsome in its new white paint, shining woodwork inside, smooth teak decks, and uniformed officers and stewards. Even more impressive was the dining room, where its newness shone in the china that had never been used and in a bewildering array of shining cutlery, unmarred by usage. At the dinner table at 7 p.m., we found fish knives and all the rest, exactly as we had been informed in Boston. You began with the utensils farthest to the left and right, and worked your way in to the plate. If, at the end of the meal, you had a few left over, unused forks or spoons, you knew you had either skipped a course or had used the wrong utensil. In the cabins we found new towels. We used the new deck chairs and noted the new life preservers. How exciting that we—the Burma missionaries—were taking this beautiful ship (never to be called a "boat") on its maiden voyage to Rangoon! We wanted to conform to life aboard ship as best we could.

That meant taking part in the ship's activities. Soon a variety of sports were organized, a ship's paper planned, a few evenings of music and dancing held on the open deck, and table games set up in the parlors. It was desirable that we cooperate. We were already "guests" in a British colony atmosphere. So we tried, although we played skittles very badly. We tried shuffleboard with better success. We threw rope rungs into the bucket and occasionally even landed one.

The other passengers were British men going out to join military and government service; wives joining husbands already there; and single men going to work in the lumber company or other commercial firms. We missionaries were in the majority, however, and sometimes a small group of us found a corner on the deck to play an American game popular at the time. It was noisy and lots of fun, but I fear it was disturbing to the other passengers. We might have been "the ugly Americans," but did not know it.

We had plenty of time for reading, writing letters to be mailed at Port Said, studying, meditating, and preparing for the task that lay ahead. Now I regret that we could not have spent some of that time studying Burmese languages. But there was no teacher and no books had been issued to us, for the particular racial group we would work with had not yet been assigned. Would it be Burmese? Karen? Kachin? Shan? The Baptist Mission had developed work in all those areas and all were crying for more missionaries. We would be assigned to one of these groups by the Burma Reference Committee, an elected body of missionaries in Burma that kept contact between Burma and the home boards.

One woman on-board was Miss Sutherland, returning to Burma for her last term of service. She had been head of a prominent Burmese girls school in Rangoon. The school took its name from Kemmendine, a suburb of the city where the school was located. I had much in common with Miss Sutherland. She knew I would be assigned to educational work, either to Kemmendine Girls School or to the equally popular Morton Lane Burmese Girls School in Moulmein. American Baptist Mission (A.B.M.) schools of various grades were located in every town of any size. Each one began on the first-grade level, but only a few continued through high school as these two schools did. Miss Sutherland, who said she wanted and needed me for the Kemmendine School, gave me much information that prepared me for working in the British educational system. By the time we reached Rangoon, I was quite ready to serve either school and psychologically prepared to cooperate with the educational system, although it was quite different from any school I had known.

During our 30 days of sailing, the first officer delighted in pointing out sights of interest. One day it was the Royal Yacht, off the coast of Portugal, taking King Alfonso into exile to England. Then the Rock of Gibraltar, a great cliff of black granite, exactly as we had seen it on the Prudential Life Insurance Company picture in our childhood. The Strait between it and Africa was unbelievably narrow. Then we were in the great Mediterranean, another sea, but a deeper blue than the Atlantic.

Now the peak of our journey—the Suez Canal—drew near. It had been officially opened with much ceremony the year after my birth. The "Big Ditch," as sailors called it, was the key to the new door of commerce for steamships to the East in the 1900s. My first journey narrowly escaped the tedious voyage of sailing ships that took five months to sail from England to the East, around Africa. Equally advantageous was our escaping the age of plane travel, which followed closely after our retirement. To be hurried in a few days from New York to Rangoon? To miss the leisurely unwinding of the ties that bind to the home base and the drawn out, eager anticipation of the adventures ahead, I think, is a loss in many ways.

A whole day and a night in Port Said was a pleasant interlude. We all stood on deck as we approached the Suez Canal entrance. The great statue, a magnificent black figure with outstretched arm pointing to the south, is called the Welcome to the East. The thrill of being so dramatically introduced to the Canal, of being so personally welcomed to the strange lands beyond as if the Canal had been dug just for me, is something I shall never forget. To relish its appeal and physical influence on the voyager, a person must come to it as I did, not knowing anything that lies beyond, having no personal knowledge of tropical climates, no certainty that you will reach the Far East, that you will like it, or that you will ever return.

At Port Said, we met with an amazing medley of races, costumes, and languages. We mailed letters, bought a few curios, but preferred the deck shopping in the shade where hawkers spread out their wares and prices changed by the hour. In the canoes and sampans that hovered around our ship another method was used. We called our choice from above, while the cooperating salesman on deck engineered the lines between us and the supplies below. Sales were made until dark. The enjoyment of a ship at anchor is a particular experience that I have always liked, if it is not too long delayed.

Also at Port Said, we packed away our coats and warm clothes and brought out summer clothing. The ship's officers changed their uniforms from dark blue to white. When going East, they reverse the procedure. The Suez Canal is the dividing line between West and East, geographically, socially, and morally.

The run through the Canal is always made by daylight "for the enjoyment of the passengers," so we were told. We found out later the real reason was for navigation purposes. Steamships sailing through the Canal had many restrictions. The Canal is narrow and without locks. In passing, one ship or the other must tie up.

Our day in the canal gave us 90 interesting miles. Within an hour, we realized we were, indeed, in a different world. The sun was hot and its glare intense. No green or trees in sight—only glistening white sand on both sides. We watched a long string of loaded camels with robed, turbaned drivers pace slowly south, and could not bear to leave the deck even for meals in the cooler dining room.

The canal marked the beginning of the last leg of the journey from Port Said to Rangoon. Passing ships, pack trains of camels, and one pitiful lonely shack to "control" Canal traffic relieved the desert sand on both sides. Later, that place became the town of Ishmalia, the terminal of a railroad to Jerusalem. In the glory of a brilliant sunset, we passed out of the Canal to the Gulf of Suez and the Red Sea, where a succession of 12 huge barren rocks—long ago named the "12 Apostles" by sailors—rises precipitously from the water.

Then we were in the lovely Indian Ocean, the most pleasant sea travel I know—as long as there is no violent monsoon storm. The rains that last from May to October were over, and though the temperature was more than warm by day, the general calm and summer weather made living delightful. At night we stood at the rail to watch the brilliance of the phosphorescent water far below us and rejoice in the rhythmic murmur of the waves at the prow of the ship. By day the flying fish amused us with their long leaps when they actually maneuvered a distance of 10–20 feet in the air by their fin-wings. We became acquainted with the southern skies, for we were sailing near the equator. Knowing that we were not likely to see some of the non-missionary friends once we were on shore, we treasured the unusual contacts. One of the young bachelors going out for the first time had been friendly with me. He seemed to have no other purpose in life than to make his mark—and his money—in the lumber business in Burma. We enjoyed many a chat by the rail. All British ships were required to hold "Divine Service" every Sunday. It was, of course, the prescribed Church of England service. The Captain led but, if he wished, he could invite an ordained passenger to conduct the service. Attendance was voluntary, but most missionaries attended. There is something about the Anglican worship that makes it particularly fitting at sea, especially the "Mariner's Hymn" which always closed the service:

"Eternal Father, strong to save,
Whose arm doth bind the restless wave,
Who bids the mighty ocean deep,
Its own appointed limits keep;
O hear us when we cry to Thee
For those in peril on the sea."

Some of the captains did not enjoy this duty of leading Divine Service or even holding it on their ships. In later years, we suspected a day's lag as we approached a port so that the confusion of landing passengers and freight took place on Sunday rather than Saturday, making Divine Service impossible.

And so it was as we approached Rangoon. The disembarkation of the *Chindwin* took place on Sunday, November 10, 1911. The approach was exciting. A great, green land! A muddy Rangoon River, palms and trees, and far on the horizon the glorious golden pagoda called Shwe Dagon and other pagodas, small and large, seen everywhere near the city. The Shwe Dagon is unique in its form, seen nowhere else except in Ceylon. The bell-shaped structure is circular at its base, rising in diminishing circular measurements to a tall, slender spire. It is not a temple or a building to be entered. It is a solid structure made of brick and cement, holy in its sacred form and worshiped as such. Pagodas in Burma are usually whitewashed. But the great Shwe Dagon is covered with pure gold.

There is always a touch of regret in leaving a ship that has so long been home. The goodbyes to the Captain and the first officer, who had been such a help to us, and the pleasant young bachelor who had tried—in vain—to convince me I was throwing my life away in mission work, were all said.

Mr. F. Phinney, the mission board representative in Rangoon, was on hand to meet us at the ship. He greeted us heartily and, looking at his list of names, relayed each piece of luggage to an elderly Indian man called Abraham. Without pencil or paper, Abraham gave a slight nod as each name was called, separated the pile of trunks, and eventually delivered them all to the Mission Press where Mr. Phinney was superintendent—and much more besides. Accommodations had been arranged for all of us. Some went as guests to private homes and some to the large Mission Guest House, actually a small hotel. Miss Sutherland took me to the Kemmendine Girls School where I stayed until the Reference Committee assigned me to a specific station and work.

I stepped ashore into a new world of heat and noise among strange people, a strange language, and strange streets and shops. With Miss Sutherland, I was introduced to a new type of transportation. An electric train line connected Kemmendine with Rangoon, but she chose to take me in a *gharry*. This private taxi was a big wooden box on four wheels drawn by a diminutive horse. The vehicle dropped lower than the high wheels. Inside we sat facing the driver on a high seat, level with the roof, though we could not see the driver. Another seat inside faced ours, and when four ride in a *gharry* the knees of each passenger touch the others'. There were side windows which could be shut against glaring sun or monsoon rains, but this day they remained open.

Kemmendine Mission School sat on a large compound of many buildings. The living apartment for the two single women in charge of the school, including a large boarding department, was on the second floor of the newest big brick building.

We were suddenly in an American home. I was given the guest room and warmly welcomed by Mrs. Elliott, a widow from Georgia finishing her first and only term of service in Burma. The rooms were comfortable and strangely familiar.

After a good dinner served by a turbaned Indian in bare feet (that troubled me), we sat in the drawing room. From now on we would use British terms for everything! While Mrs. Elliot and Miss Sutherland caught up on school matters, mutual friends in the United States, and events of Miss Sutherland's furlough, I was able to hear and to see a lot, for all doors and windows were wide open "for ventilation." That was a good idea, since warm air in motion is much easier to live with than closed-in air. On that premise, our high-ceilinged, sprawling mission homes were unscreened for many years. We had to beat the mosquito menace some other way.

I wondered how the women could talk so easily, for my ears were deafened by the terrific clatter outside. A raucous cawing of hundreds of crows filled the air as they talked over the day's scavenging in the city, before going to the rookery. Mosquitoes buzzed continually. I soon was given pillow slips to protect the few bare inches of my ankles. Burmese mosquitoes are vicious and hungry. I found they preferred rich, young blood. Their bites even penetrated cotton sleeves and net collars.

My eyes also were busy. On the wall I saw something moving, darting in and out behind a lovely framed picture of Westminster Abbey. Could it be a lizard? I was fascinated, but so disturbed by the shame of it, I tried not to notice. What would this lovely, aristocratic woman from Georgia think if she knew she had a lizard living in her beautiful parlor? How could she— how could anyone—accept living with crawling lizards in the house? I must not stare. She must not know about it.

The crows' racket finally ceased, and the warm night grew

quiet. It had been an exciting day, a wonderful day. I was in Burma! I hoped I had what it took to be a missionary.

Miss Sutherland showed me to my room and demonstrated how to sleep under a mosquito net. What a relief to see that white box as wide as the bed and six feet high, made of netting, hung from the four corner poles of the bed. The barefooted, turbaned servant, a man of about 35, yet officially called "Boy," had tucked it in under the mattress all the way around except for a small entrance spot laid loosely on the bed so I could enter, then tuck that bit in myself to be safe from mosquitoes. What comfort! Who said the missionary's life was hard? So far I had seen little of what people call "sacrifice." Lizards? Mosquitoes? Crows? Bare feet in the dining room? Not those, surely!

As Miss Sutherland left the room, she mentioned, "Coffee and toast at 6:30, and at 7 a.m. the opening meeting of this year's annual A.B.M. Conference. You will meet missionaries from stations all over Burma."

"Where?" I asked.

"On the verandah of the Rose Cottage."

"How many do you expect?" I asked.

"All who can come from the various stations, anywhere from 60 to 100," she answered.

Some verandah, I thought. I was too tired even to anticipate and fell asleep, thinking only of tomorrow. What would happen? How could any day in the future be as wonderful as this day has been! Even as I turned to sleep, a little cloud of frustration passed through my mind. How could I share this day with Edith? For five or six years were we never to laugh and talk together again? Perhaps that was the sacrifice demanded of one who answered God's call to be a missionary.

The next morning was a gift from heaven, fresh and green and promising. Not really cool, but I sensed a lessening of yesterday's heat. I heard a familiar "caw, caw" in the trees. Crows, again, with our coffee? Yes, but not as many in the morning—this is only the day crew for a small area.

A short *gharry* ride conveyed Miss Sutherland and me to the city. Here was the verandah that could comfortably seat as many local and out-station Baptist missionaries as could afford the time and expense of the trip to Rangoon. Some attended the conference only once or twice in a term. I nodded as I recognized shipmates from the *Chindwin* here and there. The opening session began with a 7 a.m. devotional meeting. The leader was an elderly man "from Loungoo," Miss Sutherland whispered to me. We sang familiar hymns and the leader made helpful comments, then called for a session of prayer. Several spontaneous prayers were given, but one more than all the others impressed me greatly. In a quiet confidence of perfect trust, he brought God's presence among us in a tangible way of the spirit. "Who is that man in the corner who just prayed?" I whispered. Miss Sutherland glanced quickly and said, "That's Clarence Chaney of Maubin." The name rang a bell. Last summer—it seemed so long ago—my friend Laura told me the tragedy that had befallen their student pastor in Irondequoit who was now in Burma! I was more impressed than ever. How could that young man, out of the agony of his tragic loss, pray like that?

The next evening, the new recruits were introduced at the Annual Reception evening of the Conference. We stood in line while everyone shook hands and welcomed us. It was a social occasion when we all dressed in our best. Even the missionaries who lived upcountry brought out their packed away nice dresses for this occasion. We, fresh from the United States, wore styles newer than theirs of four or five years earlier. This being the time and place for our best, I wore the thin, foulard silk Olive had made for me. The design was in brown and gold, the yoke and high-boned collar of brown silk net. I was glad for that dress when young Mr. Chaney of Maubin introduced himself. At once I gave him the greetings sent by Laura and the Irondequoit church. The response on his face was a winsome smile, assuring me of his happy relationship with that church. He was glad to find we had a common friend in Laura. The line passed on. I had no further chance to speak with Mr. Chaney, but I did not forget him or his prayer. Is a "sacrifice" to be demanded and accepted? In his case, it seemed both. Out of acceptance of God's will had come that prayer! I was beginning to understand what it meant to be a missionary.

Three sessions a day—reports, speeches, discussions, resolutions on mission policy passed before our astonished minds to reveal mission projects well entrenched and a living force in this land. Special committees held evening sessions after dinner relegating their problems to the Reference Committee, which met immediately after the Conference for as many days as necessary. Reference Committee members were elected by ballot posted well before the Conference date. The Reference Committee was the official body of the Conference, the channel that related the missionary administration on the field to the Boards at home. It made all assignments on the field. It handled all missionary funds for station work, and from its members had committees working continually on property, personnel, appropriations, and other areas. All votes of the Reference Committee went to the Home Boards for final approval.

One of the out-of-town missionaries was Miss Hughes from Moulmein. She and Miss Whitehead, whom I had met in Buffalo, had for many years shared the work and management as heads of Morton Lane Girls School, a combined boarding and day school. Miss Whitehead was retiring and Miss Hughes was due for furlough. She managed to convince the Reference Committee that her school needed me much more than Kemmendine did.

Lisbeth Hughes was a spinster of high spirits, British to her toes, although born in Canada. We became great friends. Her guidance and energy had brought the elementary school on through high school to a high academic level, and with a new, young helper, she aimed for the school to go even higher.

Chapter 5

TEACHING AT MORTON LANE
GIRLS SCHOOL

The Reference Committee assigned me to the Burmese work in Moulmein. For the first year, language study would be my major task in a addition to getting acquainted with the school, the church, the Christian community, and the town. Language study would continue through my second and third years, along with school responsibilities. At the end of the first year, I would appear for examination before the Language Committee of the Christian Council, which prescribed the syllabus to be studied and set the examinations for the participating missions in Burma. At the end of the third year, I would appear for the "Proficiency Examination." After that, my knowledge and use of the Burmese language would depend largely on my eagerness to learn it. Three years of study was considered merely "a good start."

When the time came for Lisbeth Hughes and me to prepare for the trip to Moulmein, I found that the red brick Mission Press building in the business district of Rangoon was the center for all mission operations both within the city and outside of it. In the storage space, we found all my luggage numbered, named, and set apart as Abraham had done at the wharf on our arrival. Now everything would be checked again, marked for Moulmein, and delivered to the railroad station.

"What language is it to be?" Mr. Phinney asked.

"I am to study Burmese," I answered.

"Then these are the books you will need. I issue them to you as a present from the Mission Press." The stack contained the Judson Bible, printed in 1840, a huge book as large as the old family Bible in my home; Judson's English-Burmese dictionary, almost as big as the Bible; Judson's Burmese grammar—a thin book of 39 pages—accepted as standard in all schools; and various tracts in Burmese, some of which I would have to translate in my first examination. "The Golden Balance" was one of the tracts, written and printed by Judson in 1820. I also received the Burmese Christian hymn book, a translation of Western Christian hymns; a primer with simple Burmese sentences such as "This is a ball" and "This is a kite"; and a convenient-sized Burmese New Testament.

It was customary for the Moulmein missionaries to make the Rangoon trip by night. Not only was it an economy of good daylight working hours, but it allowed for the two coolest parts of the day at both ends. Everyone had to have a bedroll containing a thin cotton mattress, a sheet, and a blanket rolled up in a green canvas cover. This was indispensable for all train travel. You spread it open on a flat board seat. The train trip was a rough ride with frequent stops, noisy stations, and little sleep. After having *chota-hazri* (the little breakfast of hot tea and toast) served on the steamer ferry while crossing the Great Salween River, we arrived on the Moulmein side of the river in high spirits.

The school *gharry* and some of the teachers met us. All greeted Ma Ma Hughes with the respect she deserved. She had returned triumphant bringing the new Ma Ma, who would serve the school as long and as well as she had. Or so they thought, as did I.

Like Rangoon, this, too, was a new world to me, but it was now my world. I could not hope to take it all in at once. The school building was imposing—a two-story cement building with classrooms below and dormitories above. From the entrance hall, a circular cement stairway led to the women's living quarters above and to the school offices. This also served as the entrance to the girls' dormitories. I saw at once I must be careful on those steps, for they had been worn smooth by hundreds of bare feet.

A half-dozen school teachers lived in the dormitories with the girls. I was introduced to those teachers that evening. The next morning, I met the pupils when they gathered for the 15-minute chapel service which began each school day. Here was my task. All these lovely girls. So clean, so well cared for, and so well fed! "Oh Lord," I prayed; "They are sweet. They are charming. But how can I ever tell them apart? They all look alike— black hair, black eyes, all the same delicate shade of tan, all dressed alike in colored wrap-around skirts and clean white loose jackets. All alike!" They scattered to their classes in various buildings on the compound. Each class began the day with a half-hour's Bible study. Among the day scholars and even among the boarders were many girls from non-Christian homes. Buddhist parents knew their daughters would be safe, well trained, and well educated at Morton Lane School. They gave no objection to the daily half hour of Bible study which was a definite confrontation of Christian Scriptures and faith. "It's good for them to hear," the Buddhist parents said. They never asked to excuse their daughters from attending the Bible class. But the attitude changed sharply if a 15- or16-year-old girl took it too seriously!

I was allowed to wander in and out of the classes at will, but my primary task that first year was language study. Under Miss Hughes' organization and choice of tutor, I was soon hard at it. My first teacher was an elderly Burmese gentleman, well educated in both English and Burmese. He arrived every morning at 8 a.m. His entrance and approach to my study was somewhat ceremonious. I was a bit afraid of him, and he was shocked by my mistakes. Perhaps he was afraid of me, too, for he had never before taught a foreigner to speak his language. If my halting progress was a fair sample of foreigners, I would not blame him for concluding they were a dumb lot.

But I went at it, the strangest looking language I ever saw. Its alphabet characters (script and printing alike) were made up entirely of deviations and manipulations of a perfect round circle. I had to learn to read, write, and speak. Burmese is a tonal language with nine tones to each vowel. A dot here or there, a little tail appendage above or below the circle, a little box around the circle, all are indications of tone, of meaning, of words.

Burmese is an ancient language, adapted from Sanskrit, but entirely different from all the other spoken and written languages of India. Its literature consists of the Buddhist scriptures written by stylus in "books" made of dried palm leaves. Every boy is taught to read and write his mother tongue in the monastery free school found in every village. Thus, Burma boasts the oldest public school system in the world and—at that time—the highest literacy rate of all Asia, at 50 percent. Girls had no chance of literacy before Ann Judson organized a little school for them in Moulmein. Morton Lane Girls School now had an enrollment approaching 500 students.

My dignified elderly teacher had a formality about him. His approach never varied. He paused on the threshold of the open door, made a slight bow, and asked, *"Mah-yay-lah?"* I must answer *"Mah-bah-yet,"* before he would come in and take his chair. I had to commit to memory other expressions and even Scripture verses as best I could. Gradually, I was able to speak a few sentences and even to write from dictation, but my script never fully lost its angular up-and-down stroke of English writing. My circles refused to be exactly round.

My august teacher, U Kyaw, held a government position and had to travel for a few months, so I was assigned a new teacher. U Ba Hlaing was superintendent of the Judson Boys School in town, well educated, a fine administrator, an outstanding Christian, respected and loved by the whole community. He was comfortably dignified and mature. We moved my study from the dining room to the drawing room, where tall doors opened onto a narrow, iron-railed balcony. We could actually look into some of the classrooms. Everyone in the school knew that U Ba Hlaing was the new Ma Ma's teacher. The lessons now were just as rigid in requirements, but surprisingly lighthearted, and sometimes even cheerful.

When U Ba Hlaing could no longer "spare the time" to teach me every day, my language teacher changed yet again. This time, the pastor of the Burmese church took up the job and stayed with me right through to my final examination in 1913.

Rev. L. T. Ah Syoo was Chinese to all appearances. He was tall and slim and wore Chinese clothes of spotless white: loose trousers and a hip-length long coat with standing collar. His most distinguishing mark of Chinese ancestry was his queue (pigtail) of braided black hair, which he refused to discard even after China's revolution of 1911 when queues were repudiated as "slavery" symbols imposed by the Manchus. His mother had been Burmese and his wife, Daw Mya, was Burmese. As far as I could tell, neither he nor his five brothers knew a word of Chinese. They were typical examples of how easily the Chinese became domiciled in Burma, clinging to the cherished ancestry of Kublai Khan's Empire—which included Burma in ages past— in their dress and style, yet satisfied and solid citizens of Southeast Asia. Chinese shops and stores selling staples and furniture were found in all the towns. Moulmein even had Chinese shoe-making shops. I often saw Chinese grandmothers hobbling along in their three-inch shoes.

Sunday morning at Morton Lane School was something special. All the boarders passed in line through the *port cochere,* where Miss Hughes waited on the steps. A few of the boarding teachers took turns seeing that the girls were presentable in all respects. But nothing escaped Miss Hughes' eyes. "Ma Yi, you will go back to your room to remove excess powder." "Ma Hla's hair is not neat. Do the top knot again." To me the line looked beautiful and intriguing. Even the youngest child had a little flower tucked beside her top knot. Most of the girls had lovely silk skirts they wore only on Sunday. The teachers, too, wore the same style of wrap-around skirt of delicate silks, jeweled buttons on Sunday, and the added touch of a Burmese woman's unique dress—a long flimsy scarf reaching to the knees, worn around the shoulders. This walking rainbow of color and beauty was the weekly pride of Moulmein. Two by two they walked the two blocks to the Burmese church in town. There they sat in silent devotion for an hour or more, the smallest ones in the front pews. The watchful teachers noted any sign of inattention or of unexpected situations which happened occasionally. If one of the little girls wiggled and, thereby, loosened her skirt, she quietly and naturally stood up without embarrassment to hold its width out to the right, fold it over neatly, and tuck it in tightly on the left. But when she arrived home there would be a serious talk from Sayama Dae Thir Mya telling her not to do that again. It was "not to be done in a Christian service." The alternative—losing the skirt on the way out (for all Burmese *longis* were made with no fastener of any kind)—did not seem to be relevant. Of course, even adults often had to rewrap and tighten their skirts, but it must be done inconspicuously.

When Rev. L. T. Ah Syoo stepped on the platform in his bare feet, his whole person and his dignified manner lent a devout tone to the service. Every word was in Burmese, yet the tall, erect figure in spotless white was Chinese. In this, the Burmese church asserted its legacy of the early Judson days in Moulmein when one of the first Christians to accept the "New Way" was Ah Syoo's Chinese father. Judson baptized him in a *dhobbie* (washermen's) pond as a public witness to the neighbors. This gave rise to a story told and accepted for years in Moulmein that a Christian convert was held under the water until he could see God!

Until the Japanese took control of Burma during World

War II, the church possessed the very pulpit from which Judson preached. Nothing about Ah Syoo impressed me more than his sincere humility expressed by his standing every Sunday beside the Judson pulpit, but never behind it, counting himself "not worthy" to stand where Judson had preached.

The choir gave no special numbers, but its leader, Ah Pan, with his husky voice, carried the congregation to heights of affirmation in "How Firm a Foundation." I followed the circles in the Burmese hymn book as best I could. No announcements were necessary. Every woman there knew there would be a weekly gathering in some Christian home where they would repeat one of the Christian hymns. At that meeting, women repeated verses of Scripture, sang hymns, and were further instructed in ways of Christian living, usually by Daw Mya, the pastor's wife. After a time of prayer, the women returned to their families strengthened and refreshed. Each one contributed a few pennies to the Christian work in Burma.

When I arrived in Moulmein, three ancient Burmese women who had been baptized as children by Judson himself were still alive. One was Ah Syoo's mother, who lived in their home; another was Daw Mya's mother. I was taken to see each of them so I could have a tie with Judson, who had become almost a "saint" to the Burmese church. I had one other personal touch with that man of God. Dr. Shaw Loo told me that as a young boy he had stood by the side of the road and watched as Adoniram Judson was carried on a litter to the ship, a sea voyage having been decided as a last-ditch effort to recover his health. The little boy had sensed the seriousness of the occasion by the tears of friends around him, and learned later that Judson had been buried at sea five days out in the Indian Ocean in 1850.

Moulmein was full of stories, legends, and historical facts related to the Judsons. Here Adoniram and Ann had landed in the "Golden Land" on July 13, 1813. They soon moved to Rangoon, however, and did not return to Moulmein until the British established control of Lower Burma. That was the first in a series of three conquests: 1825, 1852, and 1885, when the entire land became a British colony. The Judson compound in Moulmein included the Burmese church, the Boys School, the mission house occupied by the W. E. Wiatts when I arrived, and the A.B.M. English-speaking church. On the reasonable premise that "a new missionary needs some religious work besides language study," I was given the task of teaching a boys' Sunday school class. One boy was a great-grandson of that first Chinese convert baptized by Judson. This boy of 12 years was thoroughly Burmese—in Chinese dress.

Pastor Ah Syoo showed me another spot of the Judson story—the grave of Ann Hasseltine Judson, at Amherst, where she had sickened and died while her husband was away in Ava interpreting for the British as they signed a peace treaty with the King. Adoniram had consented to the long, slow riverboat journey to Mandalay only because he saw the opportunity to insert a clause of religious freedom for his converts into the document. Ann Judson's grave is honored and cared for by the few Christians at Amherst, a very small town at the mouth of the Irrawaddy River, 35 miles from Moulmein. The town planned there by the British never materialized, and Moulmein continued to be a useful harbor. Ann's grave bears its original white headstone. The little plot is neatly surrounded by a black iron fence, typical of the New England cemeteries of that day, as truly New England as the round, wooden pulpit in the Burmese church in Moulmein.

I had one other personal touch with the Judsons' early days. In the little Christian cemetery on the hillside are buried two of the Judson children, their little headstones giving their names and dates of birth and death: Roger died in 1815, and Maria in 1827.

My arrival in Moulmein was almost 100 years later. I found the American Baptist Mission widely spread with many avenues of Christian witness. Morton Lane School was the oldest and best known, but many other A.B.M. schools worked with full staff and hundreds of pupils. Outside the town was a school for the blind; and beyond that a center for leprosy patients. On the hill behind Morton Lane, a Mission hospital for women was being built. The missionary list for Moulmein work among tribal groups had become long. It included singles, couples, and families, and a pastor for the English-speaking community. Miss Hughes and I did not have to leave town to find companionship with other Americans. We ate together, sometimes with the other single women, sometimes in the homes of the A. J. Weekses, or the W. E. Wiatts, or the Darrows, or others.

A. J. Weeks was in charge of the missionary work among the Karen people of the district. It was a pleasant two-mile walk over the hill where the end of Morton Lane Street skirted the imposing Old Moulmein Pagoda to Daing Wun Kwin, home of the Weeks family. The school for Karen boys and girls was the town school for Christian children of the area. It was a registered government school with separate boarding departments for boys and for girls, the Karens having always accepted co-education as the Burmese did not. The Weekses had three children, and Mrs. Weeks, an artistic and talented woman, had transformed the plain, roughly built mission bungalow into an attractive home.

Mr. Weeks invited me to join him and the woman who had charge of the Karen girls' boarding department in attending the annual association of Karen churches. This was my first contact with the rural Karens. The gathering was held in the "hotter" season, when schools were closed. Burmese geographers name the seasons of Burma as Rainy (May to October), Cold (November to March), and Hot (April and May). We missionaries named the seasons differently. When asked about the climate, we said there were only two seasons—nine months of hot weather, and three months that are even hotter.

The hours traveling by river steamer were delightful, taking us into country I had not yet seen. At a riverbank landing, an ox cart waited for us. Then followed a few hours of torture, bouncing along without springs, or cover. The earth was baked as hard as stone, and the dirt track bumpy and uneven. Hamlet's "to be or not to be" was a simple problem compared to ours. To ride— showing appreciation of the courtesy given us; the discomfort of being bruised in unmentionable places of one's anatomy; the weariness of the miles; the clouds of suffocating dust—or not to ride. Walking was not much faster than riding the cart over the hard, uneven ground or over the prickly stubble of the harvested rice fields. And all under the unrelenting sun. The reward came at the end of the "ride." The warm welcome of these hundreds of Christian Karens made the trip worth it, a thousand times.

What wonderful singing! What joyous praise and thanksgiving to God, who brought them out of the primitive hilltops to the fields and rivers of this good land. We spent two days of speeches, sermons, choirs singing, prayers, and Christian fellowship. The trip gave me a window into the remarkable story of the rapid growth of the Karen churches.

On my return I realized afresh my good fortune in my post at the Morton Lane School with its cool, high-ceilinged rooms. Nights were never as hot as the days, and I had to remember the danger of getting a "chill" if I did not sleep under a light sheet. A person could live through the hot season comfortably at Morton Lane, especially when Miss Hughes and Miss Whitehead were there. They had their own little pony and trap. In the cool of the evening, the *syce,* a big bearded Indian who cared for the horses and drove the school transport for day pupils, brought the trap to the door at 5:30. After handing the reins to Miss Hughes, he jumped on the step behind us, alert to any danger or misstep of the pony. Often he shouted warnings to pedestrians in the street ahead. No one objected to this. As we passed people, they smiled, proud that the respected teachers of their children could enjoy the evening air by the harbor wall as they did.

Long before the endurance test of the hot season had passed, the pattern for "home mail" had been set. The British postal service was excellent. In cities, businesses received three deliveries a day. We were content with one daily, but we eagerly anticipated Wednesdays. That was the delivery, by night train, of the weekly mail from England, which came into Rangoon every Tuesday morning from Calcutta. The British mail had established a combination of rapid transit by using railroad service across Europe, then across India from Bombay to Calcutta. To that we Americans had to add the Atlantic crossing. Thirty days from New York was the minimum from the United States. Once that was established, Edith and I could be quite oblivious of time in our weekly letters. Every day the turbaned, barefooted Indian postman climbed the slippery stone stairs to deliver mail, but on Wednesdays it was done with a sympathetic smile and an extra *"salaam"* (greeting).

Near the end of May, clouds and winds warned us of the approach of rain, and one day the wild tempestuous southwest monsoon of the Indian Ocean suddenly swept inland. The rainy season had arrived!

With the coming of the rains, living took on a new zest. Schools opened for the new year, and once again each morning at 8:30 our compound was full of activity. The boarding girls arrived with mothers and aunts to get them settled. Hundreds of day scholars came in *gharries,* some in private conveyances that would return for them at 4 p.m. Many came by taxi service, used only when it rained. The school bus was again in service.

The temperature was still in the 80s and the humidity so high my skin was never dry. Dressing became a slow, sticky process since we wore stockings and high collars, but no one minded the rains because of the relief from the scorching heat of April. Moulmein was fairly sure of receiving 200 inches before the full moon of October, which ended the five-month period of Buddhist Lent and brought to the land its most joyous time of the year—the "Light Festival."

The downpour from the skies sometimes continued for hours, but not always. After the first erratic windy showers of May, it settled to plain rain in a more or less steady pattern. At times the water descending in perpendicular lines resembled a silver curtain outside the window through which we saw objects dimly, and I wondered how human beings could breathe in such moisture-laden air. Twelve inches falling in 11 hours was not unknown, and 14 inches in 24 hours not unusual. Gradually the brown earth became intensely green as trees and grass responded. When the earth was well soaked and fields turned to seas of thick mud, farmers with plows and oxen prepared for the long lines of workers setting rice plants by hand. Raincoats of all sorts were available for any who wanted them. They were long or short and made of a variety of material, but the quickest and cheapest were the long, dried leaves of palm and palmetto which protected only the head and back. Closed *gharries* for hire, umbrellas for some, and, years later, side curtains buckled on the high Ford cars— nothing stopped because of the rain. Its blessing was evident in the open, flooded fields where the harvest of golden rice would later feed much of Asia. Burma was assured against famine.

In the cities, scheduled meetings, concerts, and religious gatherings carried on in spite of the rain. Classes did not stop. At Morton Lane the new school year seemed busier than ever, and I spent more time in the classrooms. There was a new intensity to my Burmese study, for my first-year examination was set for November. Miss Hughes was pushing and encouraging me, knowing that to fail my Burmese examination would disgrace the whole school. Even teachers, who were quite at home in English and taught it in all the classes, began using only Burmese with me, wanting to "help" Ma Ma toward her examination.

Burmese customs were now becoming more familiar, thereby enlarging my vocabulary. At first I objected to everyone— including the dignified, elderly language teacher—addressing me as "Ma Ma." With patience and understanding, it was explained to me to be a duplicated feminine prefix. "Ma" was the first syllable of every girl's name. But when she became a teacher, as an honored and trusted elderly person, she was "Ma Ma," not the English "Mama" as I thought, although it sounded the same. I also cringed when a child making a request knelt to me. I had only to observe and listen to see how naturally and normally the children did it to all their teachers, especially if the teacher was seated, as they often were when receiving work done on slates or paper. My former pastor's words at the ship in Boston were so right: "Have patience."

When notice came that the Inspector of Schools would visit Morton Lane on a certain date, every teacher was alerted. Under the British Educational System, an inspector from the government Educational Department spent a couple of days twice a year going from class to class in all registered schools to see that the Education Code standards were being followed. Sometimes the inspector was a Burmese, but more often at Morton Lane he was an English official. The story is told that when mission schools first started and teachers were often untrained, one teacher prepared her class by saying, "If the inspector asks you 'What is the shape of the Earth?' you must say 'Round'—but it isn't; it's really flat." That day was long past.

The Morton Lane teachers of my day were all Christians and all trained as acceptable, and confirmed by grades from the government. The standards were high and the inspection thorough. At the end of the school year, a report of income and expenditure was submitted to the government, which would then remit to the school one half of the reported deficit. All the A.B.M. schools received this money, as did all other schools. Government schools—and there were many—were, of course, government supported, but no education below university level was free. School fees were set according to standards.

Miss Hughes handed over the Inspector of Schools to me so I could learn the ropes. She told the inspector that when she took furlough, I would become head of the school. The British system used the word superintendent for that title rather than the American term "principal."

As we went from class to class, the children's answers surprised me. They were well prepared. The first five minutes of every arithmetic period always began with oral mental arithmetic. The questions might be measurements of land or currency exchange. I would have needed pencil and paper and the full five minutes to reckon the answers. None of that here! Without pencil, paper, or slate, and with hands on the desk so fingers could not be used in counting, and within the half minute allowed, correct answers were given. If a head was bent over the edge of the desk, we knew the student was counting on her toes. That, too, was forbidden.

To begin algebra and geometry in the sixth grade seemed a bit much, for I had hated both in high school. We were an Anglo vernacular school, teaching English from first grade on. Even in kindergarten, Daw Thein Mya began teaching the English names of a few objects. It was her own idea (and the right one) that the earlier a child begins a foreign language, the easier it becomes. Seventh-standard examinations were all printed in English but, if a pupil wished, he or she could ask for the Burmese copy. In certain subjects, students usually preferred the English version.

The inspector and I dashed between rain showers to the wooden building of the fifth grade, where he called for a reading of the text. Conversation questions were also asked and answered. "Watch that pronunciation, Miss Northrup. The word is waas—not *wuz*." His pronunciation of the verb sounded like *waahaz*. Very well. I must accept British English and British spelling such as colour, honour, programme.

The time for my own exam approached swiftly, and my language teacher drilled me without mercy. One evening in early November, I took the night train to Rangoon. The next day I met the five kindly, elderly missionaries who formed the

Language Committee of the Mission. The exams took about three hours and covered the essentials of one year's study: reading and translating from the Gospel of John Chapter 10, writing sentences from dictation, reading a Burmese letter, and conversation with a Burman. After the committee conferred for a short time, I was listed "passed." They gave me the study regime for the next two years—a printed form and new books.

I returned to the school—and a grand welcome. I had sent a telegram and I came home a victor, which pleased every teacher, pupil, and, of course, my teacher, Ah Syoo. He avidly studied the new work, comforting himself, I think, as well as comforting me with the remark, "Well, we have two years to cover that!" My next exam would be held in November 1913. In the meantime, I would have a full schedule of work in the school because Miss Hughes would leave on furlough in April. Miss Whitehead had returned, nominally retired, but planning to live at Morton Lane until she and Miss Hughes built a little home in the cool Shan States at Taunggyi. She was willing to take over the bookkeeping and finances of the school and oversight of the Boarding Department while I became principal, in charge of the classes, the teachers, and all government relations and correspondence.

With a new young Ma Ma in charge and the elderly long-established and beloved Ma Ma Whitehead on hand to guard the girls and deal with their parents, all the teachers felt Morton Lane was in good hands for the future. Furloughs that lasted 18 months were taken in the spring. Two or three months of that time was spent on the sea voyage. There was a tender farewell held for Miss Hughes's departure and cheerful hopes for her return.

The new school year opened with the usual flock of new pupils, two new teachers, and a new superintendent studying timetables for classes and subjects. The new wing for the two-year normal school (teachers' training) had been officially opened with due ceremony before Miss Hughes left. Those classes now came under my supervision as well. From 9 a.m. to 4 p.m., my days were spent either in the classrooms or in the office. My language study continued; one hour in the morning with my teacher, one hour in the evening by myself, and as much other time as I could find.

My sleeping room, and the only room I ever had at the school, was a makeshift bedroom divided from the office by a curtain. My work area was on the office side, where the big roll-top desk was in constant use. Miss Whitehead sat there, dispensing money to the boarders from their allowance as provided by parents and the school cash for various bills. One time I lay in bed behind the curtain for three days with fever. Dr. Ah Pon, the school physician, cared for me as he did for the girls. It happened to be the end of the month when the teachers received their pay. Paper money had not yet come into general use. It was a custom that all silver *rupees* (coins) must be tested by holding one in the left index finger and striking it on the edge of an already tested one. The result was a clear metal ring if the silver was "pure." The payroll was nearly 900 *rupees* and, as that little metallic click went on endlessly, it seemed each one rang through my aching head. This was an endurance record I had not anticipated when I signed on to be a missionary.

All letters for the girls passed through Miss Whitehead's hands, and she often passed them to me for my practice in Burmese. If it should happen—and it often did—that the letter was from a boy other than her brother, Miss Whitehead destroyed it, saying, "If her father knew about this, he would take his daughter out of our school at once." The girls were under her protection, and she gladly gave it, for she did not intend to interfere with Burma's social customs. Once, however, she showed me a letter from a boy in the Government High School. He had in some way found out that his love notes to pretty Ma Hla were not reaching her, so he boldly directed a letter of protest to the "Big Ma Ma" at Morton Lane. It was in English, of a sort, and he was evidently a Christian, though his spelling was poor when he bluntly asked, "Where does it say in the Bibble [sic] that boy must not love girl?" He made his point, but even that did not melt Miss Whitehead's heart. She was not ready for any hint of change in the Burmese customs of segregation by sex of school children. The subject was raised at a school board meeting: "Why should the mission take on the expense of two high schools in Moulmein? Why not co-education like the Karens?" Miss Whitehead replied, "If that day comes, I shall resign at once. I would not take that responsibility for the girls."

The living apartment for the missionary women at Morton Lane consisted of only a dining room behind the school office and a small pantry for serving the food. The kitchen, called "the cook house," was on ground level, far removed from our dining room on the second floor. The cook had to manage a long flight of stairs in the open. We could hardly expect the soup to be hot. There was also a good-sized drawing room where we sat in the evening. It was accessed from the dining room by a corridor beyond the office. Knowing my love of music, Miss Whitehead added a piano to the room.

The boarders did not have private rooms in their dormitories. They each had a bed, a small space for dressing, the floor mirror for their elaborate hair-do's, and space for the small metal box in which all extra clothing was stored folded flat. Every room had 20 beds on each side, all at right angles to a middle corridor through the long room. Some girls had bed nets. There was no closed ceiling above them. Roofs rested on rafters and girders requiring brooms 15 feet long to sweep down the cobwebs. Windows stood wide open, and the evening sea breeze from the harbor gave good ventilation. There were four dormitories of this type, all on the second floor. In each room there were at least two corner "rooms" for teachers, who had curtained privacy while vigilantly keeping watch over the girls. Miss Hughes and Miss Whitehead used such corner rooms as their bedrooms and had no others during all their years at the school. There had once been a third room to the office apartment, but it had to be used as a sick room for boarders.

Home mail day continued to be the bright spot of the week and, during all my years abroad, Edith's regular letters never failed more than a half-dozen times, nor did mine to her. She and Father were discovering many things to enjoy together. Her music teacher had found a place for her in the violin section of the Rochester Symphony Orchestra. Father's old violin on which I remember his playing by ear, now laboriously followed the prescribed notes. But Edith loved playing, and in a few years fell in love with the cornet player.

It was clear that she did not understand my environment, and I purposely did not relate what I thought she could not accept. What I did inadvertently write one time caused her shocked comment, "Have you been keeping things from me? Tell me truly, when you go out walking do you have to meet men *(coolies)* without shirts on?" Not until my second furlough did I dare tell her about the little lizards on the walls in our houses.

"Where are they?" she asked gingerly.

"On the walls—anywhere," I said. It was time for her to learn. And I added a bit of information I had carefully withheld. "And sometimes," I said, "they fall!"

In a tone of horror, she asked, "Where? Where do they fall? Do they fall on you?"

They never had at that time, but I answered, "They could." I added truthfully, "And sometimes when one falls, its tail breaks off! It doesn't matter," I said, "they scamper back up the wall and in time grow a new tail."

The distressed look on Edith's face warned me that I had gone too far for reasonable credence. She was silent, and we never discussed the little geckos again. But years later for a bit of fun, she would begin a letter, "Well, Elsie, who swept up the tails this morning?" The geckos' broken tails became a family joke. I doubt if they ever believed my true story.

Chapter 6

MEETING MR. CHANEY

The year 1913 was outstanding in Burma, marking the centennial of the Judson's arrival in the Golden Land. Special meetings were scheduled in Rangoon and Moulmein with Board
members and American friends in attendance. The beginning of
the work in Burma had been extremely slow, while back in
America the few missionary-minded Baptist churches were so
eager for "results" (meaning "reported converts of the hea-
thens"). At the end of the first seven years, Adoniram Judson
received a cable inquiring, "What are the prospects?" His reply
has ever since been the motto for Christian missions: *"The
prospects are as bright as the promises of God."* In the very next
year, the first Burmese convert—U Naw—was baptized, and
with a few missionaries the first Baptist Church in Rangoon was
organized. Now, 100 years later, the Burma Baptist Convention
prepared to greet the American visitors.

The 1913 Judson Centennial had been planned for and
talked about for more than a year. Special meetings would be part
of the annual all-Burma Baptist Convention held in Rangoon in
November. Members of both of the American Baptist Mission
Boards, representatives of other missions, and many Baptist leaders from the United States attended. They thrilled to the
"promises of God" fulfilled as hundreds of Christians from all
sections of Burma arrived. They were astonished by the singing,
the choirs, the radiant faces, and the poise and intelligence of the
Karen and Burmese leaders. Historical records of the Judson days

were reiterated and a pageant written and performed by the Christians themselves.

My language teacher, Pastor Ah Syoo, performed the role of greatest honor—the part of Adoniram Judson. The pastor, who always wore spotless white, was dressed as Judson, a prisoner of the Burmese king. We saw him dirty, unkempt, in rags, sitting in the empty lion's cage where he was allowed a little fresh air each day from the foul, crowded prison.

After the convention, the American visitors spent two days in Moulmein. There was so much of the Judsonian atmosphere, so many mission projects to interest them, that the pilgrimage to visit Ann's grave at Amherst had to be canceled. Among the visitors, I was delighted to find Charles Tenny, son of my former Sunday school teacher in Hilton, and Mr. Traver, the current pastor of Hilton Baptist Church. I again met Mrs. H. G. Safford, the Foreign Secretary of the Woman's Board, with whom I had my first contact at the Board meeting in Buffalo. She would be in Burma visiting projects of the Woman's Board for two or three months.

Perhaps the most unforgettable experience in Moulmein for the American visitors was the afternoon they met two elderly women who had been baptized by Judson. They were helped to the platform, where they sat a few minutes in front of the audience. They did not speak, and only a few of us knew why one of them kept her hands hidden under a silk scarf. She had leprosy, but was still being tenderly cared for in her Christian home.

It had been hoped that Pastor Ah Syoo's mother would also sit on the platform at the celebration, but she died shortly before the Centennial. I had met her in 1910 and later attended her funeral. I had not attended many funerals in the United States, but when I did they exuded sorrow and sadness. Custom demanded black clothing, quiet whisperings, tears, and regrets. At the cemetery the slow painful procession to the grave was equally pathetic. I remembered my mother's funeral, when Olive walked with Father behind the coffin. Edith and I followed in tears, and my uncontrollable weeping interfered with the black veil I had to wear over my face. I remember nothing cheerful about that funeral. Yet we were Christians!

Pastor Ah Syoo's mother's funeral was a mighty witness to the Christian claim of immortal life. Miss Whitehead gave me a note which had been brought to the school: "Our mother has gone home to her Lord. We want to make this a joyous occasion that will show our non-Christian neighbors our faith. Please arrange for 12 or 15 of the best singers in the school to come early to the church." When the hour for the service arrived, the group of Morton Lane schoolgirls stood at the front entrance singing:

> *"The Homeland, the land of the free born,*
> *There's no death in the Homeland*
> *But only glorious morn."*

Inside the church, the choir sang songs about heaven. Pastor Ah Syoo stood as usual on the platform beside the Judson pulpit. With love, respect, and great dignity, he gave tribute to his mother, telling of her long Christian life and her Christian home and family. After the benediction, her six sons gathered and carried her to her grave. They were well-known men in Moulmein, and their names read like a poem: Ah Syoo, Ah Sou, Ah Pan, Ah Pon, Ah Cho, and Ah Seong. The funeral was not the only witness this Christian family gave to non-Christian neighbors. A death or funeral was, by Burmese tradition, more than a family affair. Every friend and neighbor was entertained in the home for three evenings following the funeral. The program included refreshments, speeches, and a chance to see old friends and to hear this strange doctrine of life after death explained by preachers. All good entertainment! When the guests went home, they talked it over among themselves.

"Did you hear what they said—life after death?"

"Incredible."

"But they believe it!"

"How can they?"

"But they do! They believe."

And sometimes the wistful expression, "It would be so wonderful if it were true."

"Yes, let's find out about it."

The seeds had been planted; God would give the increase.

The year 1913 was outstanding for the Chaneys, too. During the monsoon rains, Mr. Chaney and I began a casual exchange of letters. The letters were not from me; they were from Laura. As soon as she heard I had met Clarence Chaney, she wanted him to know the church in Irondequoit had not forgotten him and even hoped he would return there. I passed that word on to Mr. Chaney. I added a few lines, knowing he had no social outlet other than occasionally eating dinner with two elderly missionary women who lived nearby. My sister Edith and I exchanged voluminous letters, and I felt sorry for anyone who did not have an outlet for sharing all the new experiences of living in a different country.

It wasn't surprising then that Mr. Chaney wrote back, especially when he had some excitement to share. He wrote about the state dinner given by the District Commissioner of Maubin in honor of the coronation of King George V. A few officials had been called to attend, and as representative of the Christian community, Mr. Chaney also was invited, although he was American. Anglican clergy often wore the round, high white collar which opens in the back, with a plain, high black vest. Mr. Chaney and some others of the American Baptist Mission decided that outfit would be suitable for such an occasion. To this, Mr. Chaney added his Prince Albert coat, commonly worn in the pulpit at that time. It was his best, and he went to the dinner feeling not only well dressed, but also relieved in spirit because "Good King George," as he was later called, had given word to the Empire that the toast to the King no longer need be made with strong liquor. The toast could be raised in any beverage, even water.

When Mr. Chaney arrived at the site of the function, his host met him at the top of the stairs. The host shook Mr. Chaney's hand, saying, "Good evening, Padre," and reached for the Prince Albert coat. With as much grace as possible, Mr. Chaney clung to his coat, trying to make the man understand he wore only shirt sleeves beneath it. The host quickly sized up the situation and passed the guest on to meet a dignitary from Rangoon. The awkward moment passed, and I had a good laugh over Mr. Chaney's letter explaining the social *faux pas*.

Mr. Chaney's occasional notes were interesting, and I shared them with Miss Whitehead. He wrote about a new motorboat, the gift of two Chaney uncles, which would ease his touring season in the delta. Previously, he wasted a lot of time when he had to wait for boats and rowers who depended on the tides. Now he was independent of tides and could visit twice the number of villages. He named the boat for the two uncles: *Harry Morris*. Mr. Chaney needed some special instruction about the engine, however, and accepted an invitation from the Wiatts to visit them in Moulmein for a couple of days.

During that visit, I joined the Wiatts and Mr. Chaney on a delightful launch ride up the river. Both evenings after school, Mr. Chaney and I walked on the hill ridge behind Morton Lane. It did not appear strange to me that this lonely young man sought the companionship of someone near his own age. As time went on, whenever I had to go to Rangoon on school business, Mr. Chaney also had errands there. We were friends, and I thought we could keep a delightful interest in each other on that basis. But if mission gossip coupled our names, it would embarrass both of us. So we held our picnic chats in places where missionaries did not usually go—the upper open platform of Shwe Dagon Pagoda, for instance. One time he surprised me by inviting me to lunch at the Strand Hotel. We found much of common interest in our Rochester, New York, backgrounds. His relationship with the two congregations at Irondequoit had taken a strange turn. Learning there was no hope of his returning as pastor, they decided to join denominations other than those of the majority of members so that no one could ever say, "We always did it that way!" The result? The Baptist student pastor unwittingly fathered two churches in Irondequoit: one Congregational, the other Presbyterian. On furlough, he preached at both by request, and found himself among friends.

As the year progressed, Clarence's letters took on a new tone. He mentioned the joys of comfortable evangelistic tours in the *Harry Morris,* two and three weeks at a time. But there was a new note of urgency, of wanting to see me, suggesting we should get to know each other better and anticipating our next meeting. After the hot season, we met, spending a few hours in some sheltered spot—at the pagoda or at the Royal Lakes, where we ate our picnic lunch under the roof of an open summer house while the monsoon rains poured in sheets on the ground around us. I was getting to know this man of integrity. His warm interest, personal attention, and—most of all—his downright goodness, revealed to me a heart of gold, which drew me to him. He never made any plea for pity. The tragedy of his first year in Burma was never mentioned, although he did speak of Eastman, the little son in his grandmother's care in Massachusetts. Clarence sometimes referred to him with longing, for he had never known him other than as a motherless baby.

In September, Clarence wrote that he had an errand in Moulmein and would again be a guest of the Wiatts. We had long walks and long talks on the ridge above the town. I learned about his background. Clarence was born on June 5, 1878, in Rockford, Illinois. He spent his early boyhood in Rockford and Ravenswood (in Chicago). His mother died when he was nine, and by the time he was thirteen, Clarence's home was broken up. He spent several years working on farms in Iowa and Indiana.

Then he returned to school, seeking an education worthy of a minister of the gospel. In 1903, he graduated from the Mount Hermon School for Boys (one of D. L. Moody's Northfield Schools) in Massachusetts. He earned his B.A. at Yale and a B.D. degree from Colgate-Rochester Divinity School. He was ordained in the Baptist church in New Haven, Connecticut, and married Louise Hinds Eastman, who died in April 1910. He arrived in Burma in 1909.

When Clarence added to his admiration and respect, his love, I could not turn from it, for I knew his whole being was behind it. On the last morning before he left Moulmein, I gave Clarence my promise. He would meet me in November when I went to Rangoon for my final language examination. We would talk over future plans then. There would be no publicity of an engagement before Christmas. This delay was timed to the slow mail; I wanted my father and sister to be the first to know of my changed plans.

I no longer shared Clarence's letters with Miss Whitehead, although they passed through the office mail. She became less friendly, clearly disapproving of what she feared. I could not tell her, and it would not have comforted her if I had. This possible change in my plans would terribly upset her plans and the assured future of the school. She could not help but see what was inevitable. But I knew this relationship was God's plan for my life and service in Burma. Clarence persuaded me that, as his wife, I would have even greater scope and opportunities to be a missionary, for I could combine both education and evangelism.

Then another blow descended on the Morton Lane School. Lisbeth Hughes sent word that she could not return to Burma as expected. For health reasons, her furlough must be extended.

The influence of the mission schools in the growth and development of the church in Burma can hardly be exaggerated. In that respect Morton Lane stood high. Its whole atmosphere and teaching was definitely Christian, individually and personally. All the teachers were Christians. Although a large percentage of the girls came from Christian homes, some of the boarders and many of the day students were Buddhists. All of them conformed to the religious instruction given by attending daily Bible class and Sunday church services. I remember no case of parents asking for exemption. We put no pressure on the Buddhist students to change their religion, but the evidence all around them of the joy and blessing of the Christian faith could not be restrained. It had its own appeal, for it was Truth in its essence, though often inadequately and poorly represented by its humble followers.

Hundreds of girls who dared not risk the disapproval of Buddhist parents were believers in Christ in their hearts all their lives. Only rarely was there a belligerent, defensive Buddhist student such as Ma Nyunt, who went from bed to bed after lights out and whispered, "Don't let them make a Christian out of you." She did not understand, poor child! We did not attempt to "make" Christians. The aim of missions is to spread the Good News of salvation of a loving God, a Creator, and a Savior. Any response to that must be personal and voluntary. Out of the response of students to the gospel message has come the strong national church in Burma. The mission schools also gave the church its educated leadership.

Any girl who spent even a few years at Morton Lane received excellent Bible knowledge and religious training. The students knew the hymns and the order of Christian worship. They were familiar with prayer, having heard short, spontaneous prayers from Christian teachers six times a day: thanks at morning rice, and prayer at chapel, at Bible class, at evening rice, at evening study hour, and at bedtime.

My final language examination took place in November 1913. If I passed, this would end my three-year study with a tutor. The night train from Moulmein arrived in Rangoon at 5:30 a.m. Clarence was on the platform to meet me. We had toast and coffee at the station, then checked in at the Mission Guest

House. I had reserved that day for study, so not until evening did we have a chance to visit, and very little time even then. "Let me get this exam off my mind first," I begged.

The Language Committee consisted of five elderly missionaries—all men. Various aspects of the Burmese language were tested in turn. It took nearly all day, for I was "not to be nervous or hurried," so they said! I had to write a paper answering 10 out of 12 questions that would indicate my thought pattern in Burmese. Next I wrote a long Burmese letter on a list of suggested subjects and translated another letter I had never seen from Burmese into English. Sentences were dictated for me to write, with special care over spelling. Sections of the Burmese New Testament were given to me for immediate translation. One of the prescribed texts for the exam was a favorite story from the Buddhist scriptures written in high, literary Burmese. A short section of this piece was given me for translation along with a portion from Adoniram Judson's tract "The Golden Balance." There was a set of questions on Burmese grammar, and last—and worst—I had to speak for five minutes on a subject I might choose from three handed to me, with only five minutes to collect my thoughts. I chose one related to schoolwork, which I knew best. I had several things to say, but eventually ran out of remarks. Finally, in desperation, I stopped and addressed the kindly old man sitting directly in front of me. "Haven't I talked for five minutes yet?" He pulled out his watch and said, "Oh yes, much more than five minutes! I was so interested in what you were saying I forgot to look at the time." Late that evening, the committee reported, "Miss Northrup has passed her Proficiency Burmese examination with credit" (which meant an overall average of more than 90%).

With the relief of my exam passed, Clarence and I had a most happy visit the next day. We determined that the great work to which we were both dedicated must not suffer because of our personal plans. After much prayer and deliberation, we decided that since Miss Hughes was not returning as expected and a new missionary must be found to take my place at Morton Lane, the Board would need a full year to find a substitute. Therefore, we would not ask for my release until November 1914. Clarence had not yet had a furlough and was in poor health, so we planned to ask if he could go to America in June 1914. In the meantime, he would continue a full evangelistic touring season lasting from December to March. We also made plans to spend the hot season at the same hill station. All of this, of course, would have to be presented to the Reference Committee in Burma for their approval and then forwarded to the mission Boards at home. That was Clarence's duty!

While I had been working through my exam, he had gone shopping in the bazaar. An Indian diamond dealer had insisted Clarence take with him a half-dozen unset stones to "show the lady," and part of the fun that day was to decide on a stone. This was a rare experience. Unset jewels were common trade items with both Indians and Burmese, and surprisingly cheap. A reliable dealer warmed to Clarence, and the small stone of perfect cut which we agreed on was a beauty. The clever goldsmith quickly set it in a ring that fitted perfectly, and I returned to Moulmein with two treasures—an engagement ring and a "Pass with credit." There was great rejoicing in the school over the pass. The ring was locked away for Christmas.

Before that event, calamity hit the Maubin mission. I started to read the letter about it to Miss Whitehead, but she had become so antagonistic to me (probably not so much to me personally as much as to my future plans, which she judged as inexcusably selfish). She refused to listen, shut her office desk with a bang, and walked out of the room. I can understand the hopes for the school that she had built up with me there. Now those plans were ruined. Her whole life had been given to that school. She and Lizbeth Hughes had long planned their retirement in Burma's cool Shan State. It comforts me to know that circumstances did make their plan possible, and they spent some years there in their own pretty, stone house.

The calamity involved the mission house in Maubin. It had been built 50 years earlier, and Clarence lived in it for more than four years. The house had a magnificent view of a great sweep of the Irrawaddy River where, on its curve, was located the town of Maubin. Many river steamers passed daily. But the house was built on the riverbank in front of the *bund* (levee) which protected the other mission buildings from floods. The heavy monsoon rains and the swollen river had eaten away the bank. One day when Clarence returned home from the school at 4 p.m., he found Appia, the household helper, sweeping the front verandah of his house. Clarence noticed a decided slant to the floor, but Appia hardly stopped his sweeping to say, "Master's house falling down." And so it was!

Calling school boys to help move things out, Clarence supervised the demise of the old mission house. Within an hour, a great section of the bank washed into the Irawaddy River, and in its place—300 feet long and 100 feet wide, where once the house had stood—Clarence found 20- to 30-foot-deep water. The house was turned into a raft of broken teak boards. Much of this fine wood was salvaged, and Clarence built a neat little one-room cottage out of the old lumber. The *Harry Morris* rode at anchor where the former house once stood.

It was Morton Lane's turn to host the Moulmein Christmas missionary dinner in 1913. The long table had to be set in the office room, for there were 17 of us to enjoy this feast, the one time of the year when all the missionaries gathered together. Apart from one couple who worked among the Anglo-Indians, an English-speaking community, the rest of us spoke a variety of languages in our work. Once in a while, we enjoyed using English. We were a congenial party. The special dinner had been carefully planned and prepared. The cook and the serving boys wore their best white uniforms. They were as happy as we were, for Christmas meant special bonuses for them, although not all of them were Christians.

My ring was hidden in my lap until dessert. Then the group was told to turn over their place cards and work out the puzzle on the back—a jumble of letters in a long, unbroken, unknown word. While they studied it, I slipped on my ring. Soon Mr. Darrow said, "I can find Chaney in it," and with that clue, it was not long before they had found my name, too. Mr. Wiatt commented on a "new light" at the table as my ring flashed its message. Lest there be anxiety for the work (always a concern in mission plans), I shared our plans by which Clarence would leave for a much-needed furlough but I would not leave until the following November. We would be married at home before returning to Burma. This surprised and pleased them all except Mr. Darrow, who questioned the wisdom and my placid acceptance of letting Clarence "go home" without me, putting half a world between us! Perhaps he did not know Mr. Chaney as I had come to know him, and could not share my complete confidence in Clarence's integrity and his deep committed love. None of us anticipated our separation by World War I.

Mr. Darrow was not the only one who expected a marriage much sooner. Some of the American Centennial visitors were still in Burma, touring the upcountry mission stations. Among them was Mrs. H. G. Safford, Foreign Secretary of the Woman's Board. She had always had a special interest in me and my appointment. Engagements in the mission were rare, and our news reached her quickly. Her's was one of the first letters I received after the announcement. She raised no question of my change of plans, though she, more than anyone else on the Woman's Board, would be involved in the loss to one of the Board's pet projects. She wrote a warm letter of blessing, but reminded me of the importance of the school and "hoped I would not leave before the end of the school year in March."

How grateful I was that Clarence accepted my desire to

delay our marriage by a full year or more. Neither of us was young, and he had endured more than four years of depressing loneliness, yet for the sake of the Lord's work, Clarence yielded all claims he might have made. Mrs. Stafford returned to the United States long before Clarence did, and if there was need to pacify the Board members, we knew she was in full sympathy with our plans.

The memorable evening was not yet finished. I asked the boarding teachers to gather in one of the curtained corner rooms after dinner because I had something important to say to them. The teachers had all the privileges of living in the house and were a tremendous asset to the school. Daw Shive Hme was the eldest. She had lived there almost as long as Miss Whitehead, and when any serious problem in the Boarding Department arose, it was referred to her. By her long years of devoted service and even more by her dignity and quiet, warm-hearted manner, she endeared herself to the girls. Without any self-seeking, she acquired authority that often smoothed issues of discipline before they reached Miss Whitehead's attention.

I found the group impatiently waiting, and at once told them the news and showed my ring. I was going to marry Mr. Chaney of Maubin. Of course they had seen him in Moulmein several times. Some had studied Bible courses with him at summer conferences. They were quite ready for a romance and confessed they had "wished it" on me. Yet they all had the interests of the school at heart and were troubled until I told them I would remain with them until the following November, when they would have a new Ma Ma. They beamed with joy and shared my happiness. Dainty little Ma Saw Hman, the music teacher, expressed their pleasure and love for Mr. Chaney by calling him Ko Ko (big brother) Chaney, which became Clarence's name at Morton Lane. Only Daw Shive Hme could hardly understand, and said to Miss Whitehead, "What has happened? We have had many different Ma Ma's here; this never happened before!" Whether Miss

Whitehead took that as a compliment or not, I never knew, but whenever it was mentioned she reflected almost sadly, "This never happened here before!" Something had gone wrong in her universe.

The school inspection that last quarter was severe. Mr. Wedderspoon himself, the Superintendent of Public Instruction, led it. He stayed at the Government Guest House at Martaban, arriving by ferry each morning spotlessly groomed and fresh for the day's work. He checked the subjects, the teachers, and the pupils. The Government Education Department issued final examinations yearly, but only for seventh grade and the final grade of high school. Heads of schools were asked to mark the papers. When Clarence and I accepted the invitation to spend our vacation in April and May at Sinlum Kaba, in the Kachin Hills, part of my luggage was a big wooden box of 200 examination books in geography. I had to mark these and send a report to the Education Office in Rangoon.

By long-established custom, vacationers in the hill stations worked in the mornings, rested and played in the afternoons, and spent evenings outdoors or visiting and playing games inside. Missionaries who lived year round in the hill stations graciously opened their homes in April to workers who lived most of the year in the hot climate.

When the missionaries from the hills took their vacations in the cities in the winter, we lowland dwellers reciprocated. The interest in the Northrup-Chaney engagement brought Clarence and me more than one invitation. We accepted the one from Bhamo. It meant a fairly long train ride and a final climb to an altitude of 6,000 feet on ponies. Sinlum Kaba was really a Christian Kachin village. Nearby, our mission maintained a grass-roofed guesthouse. In the evening, bundled in coats and sweaters, we sat outdoors till the evening light on the great Irrawaddy River, far below us, faded to darkness. The sensation of feeling "cold" was part of the pleasure.

Clarence and I were not the only guests. Besides the host and hostess, missionaries from Mandalay and Loungoo brought new interests, and the conversation often turned lively. Clarence and I kept our afternoons together, taking my sewing and our books to a lovely spot beside a gentle waterfall. We now had time not only for plans but also for introductions to each other's families. He had already met my father and Edith by his letter of courtesy to my father—the traditional "request" for a daughter—and had won them both. They entered naturally into our conversations. I learned about Uncle Harry and Uncle Morris and other Chaney relatives, and for the first time we began using our first names to each other, but not in front of the others. Mr., Mrs., and Miss were continued in the whole mission until long after World War I and, in some cases, never discontinued. When, later, the tendency to refer to each other by the more familiar first names began in the English Wesleyan Mission, it was strictly forbidden by the head office. We had long walks and, occasionally, if the ponies were not hauling firewood or rice, slow rides over the foot trails. Clarence's sailing date had been set in June. Whenever we referred to that parting, the disturbing thought was softened when he added in a vigorous tone, "and you will come in November." No question about that, I thought. How little did we know of the conditions that would separate us!

All the vacationing missionaries attended the Sunday service in the village, though none of us, except our host, spoke Kachin. In Asia, a Christian becomes almost indifferent to the language of worship and can sit comfortably through an hour of preaching in a strange tongue, knowing his presence is a witness to the God he serves. In Asia you see so much "worship" in so many forms that you become indifferent to language and respectful of "worship" as such—a mystical urge of man that leads him to the state of longing, of yearning, and of self-negation that is worship. This is not quickly recognized nor understood by the Westerner, for it is spiritual only and seems far removed from the immediate environment. It is the universal sign that man is more than a physical being. Of course the only complete and satisfying worship is to find God and His revelation in Jesus Christ. That is the urgency for missions, for witness at home and abroad, the answer to the questions raised in Romans 10:14: *"How then shall they call on Him in whom they have not believed? and how shall they believe in Him of whom they have not heard? and how shall they hear without a preacher?"*

The Kachins were more primitive than the Karens, and mission work among them began much later. This area of upper Burma was held under the Burmese King until 1885. When two Baptist missionaries were presented on their knees before King Thee-bau, requesting permission to preach among the Kachins, he spurned their request, saying, "You can as easily teach a dog to read as a Kachin." Yet in 1913, we saw a school in the village, a trained preacher in the pulpit, and held a Kachin hymn book (printed at the A.B.M. Press in Rangoon) in our hands. We could sing along because the translation of Scripture for the Kachins had introduced a new medium. Instead of adapting the Burmese alphabet of circles as had been done for the Karens, the Kachin language had been Romanized, and we could read the strange sounds in English-looking words. They were strange sounds indeed. How do you pronounce Kwyouk, and what did it mean? Never mind; sing it. The tune is familiar. So we joined their Christian praise and thanked the translator for giving the Kachins a readable language.

I carefully marked the geography exams and sent the report to the Director of Public Instruction (D.P.I.) in Rangoon. But what was I to do with the big heavy box of papers? I had no instructions, and dared not destroy them. So I asked the D.P.I. what to do with them. I received what was probably the shortest official letter ever sent. It was on full-sized legal paper, and said:

Burn 'em
I have the honour
to be, Madame,
Your most obedient servant
G.W.

In May it was time to return to the hot plains. My host asked me to take along two Kachin girls who were ready to finish their education in the Kemmendine Girls School. They were in for a big adventure. At school they would have to learn both Burmese and English. They had never seen a train before, but preserved the stolid, oriental expression and showed no surprise. I could not talk with them, for I knew no Kachin. Trains in Burma were not in a hurry. They stopped often and stayed long at the stations. Passengers roamed from one carriage to another to visit with friends. The girls and I were situated in one compartment and Clarence in another. He spent a few hours with us each day, and he and I referred to the girls as our chaperones.

Neither of us lingered in Rangoon, since the monsoon rains were due. Schools would open, and all must be ready for the next year's work. By June the schools would be operating at full steam, and I would come to Rangoon for Clarence's sailing. Miss Whitehead had experienced a change of heart and was glad to see me back. My language teacher was interested in my plans but worried for fear that all his work—and mine—be "lost," because the language in the area where Mr. Chaney worked was Pwo Karen. His fear proved ungrounded. All the Karens who lived in the delta area spoke Burmese fluently. Only in their religious language did they cling to their ancestors' Karen. The church services were always conducted in Karen on that field.

By the time I was due in Rangoon again, I was burdened with long shopping lists. Teachers wanted new books for certain classes, new equipment, new hymn books, and much more. All that could wait until Clarence and I said our goodbyes at the

Guest House. I did not want to see the ship leave, and did not go
to the jetty. Dr. and Mrs. McCurdy, of our mission, were sailing
on the same ship. When Clarence wrote that he and Dr.
McCurdy had climbed to the top of the Great Pyramid, with a
guide behind to push and one in front to pull them up, I was glad
they were traveling together.

The Henderson Line ships from Rangoon to Liverpool
made one stop in Port Said. Our world had no phones and no
radio contact with ships at sea. Nineteen days elapsed before
Clarence could mail his first letter. By adding the quickest return
post possible, my calendar was marked for that Wednesday—
home mail day! It was a long wait. When I hurried from a classroom to the office and looked through the mail Miss Whitehead
had laid on my desk, I found no letter in Mr. Chaney's hand-
writing. I was stunned. No letter? It couldn't be! All that day and
much of the night, I was troubled. I shared none of Mr. Darrow's
apprehensions. Had something happened to Clarence? To the
ship?

When I came to the office the next day, Miss Whitehead
said, "I had to sign for this parcel to you." I opened the parcel to
find 19 separately dated letters—one written each day between
Rangoon and Port Said. All was well! Clarence explained his
plan: he would rest a few days in Egypt, then sail to Italy, and
finally take a direct crossing to New York. I could now begin
sending letters to the Eastman home in Mt. Holyoke. Clarence's
letters were full of love, anticipation, and happiness.

The routine of the new school year of 1914 was now familiar to me—the chatter of the girls, the joy of the teachers to be
back again, the visits of the parents, the happiness of the students
except for a few homesick girls in the dormitory. That would
soon pass as they responded to the kindness and mothering of the
teachers.

My official school duties were pleasant to me now. Yet all this
was to end in November, in just a few more months. At times I

felt dismay, wondering if I could possibly be as happy in Maubin as I had been in Moulmein. But happiness was not an issue if I was to be a missionary, and I remembered Clarence's insistence that I would be "more a missionary" working with him than under the limitations of school life. I would find my heart melting to Clarence's goodness, his integrity, his devotion, and his love. All this was waiting for me. It was God's gift to us both.

For the first time, Morton Lane had a male teacher on its staff: Ah Sou, one of the "Chinese" Ah family, taught art classes, relieving Ma Saw Hman to give more time to the music classes. We had all admired Au Sou's talent. He painted with oils on silk and had given me a wide, knee-length silk scarf with a gorgeous "Peacock in Pride," the national emblem of Burma, on both ends. This scarf was the crowning touch of my beautiful Burmese costume. At Christmastime we all loved Ah Sou's cards—lovely river scenes, pagodas, and bamboo homes painted in delicate watercolors.

My carved teak chest now became a "hope chest" which I filled with fine tea cloths, lace doilies, and beautiful Irish damask linen ordered directly from Ireland. I invited the teachers to see how an American girl prepared for her marriage and new home. I doubt they were much impressed with cloth instead of jewels.

Chapter 7

FIGHTING IN THE WORLD

Moulmein was well on its way to its usual 200 inches of rain in five months when the bomb struck—literally. Our only source of news was the Rangoon daily newspaper, which arrived by the night train. The headlines read, "War!" "War in Europe!" "Fight for England." Of course, we Americans were not involved. We were "neutral." But Burma was a British colony; its citizens were members of the British Empire. The date was August 4, 1914, and Clarence and I were separated by half the world. At my last news he was waiting in Italy for a ship to take him to New York.

Soon the Burmese teachers heard the shocking news. They came to Miss Whitehead and me full of questions. What about this war? Why? Where? What was "a war" anyway? When the news contained accounts of actual fighting, the teachers asked for explanations. "Why do they fight on Sunday? Don't they worship God on Sunday as we do?" We had no satisfying answers. We hesitated to tell them of the madness and cruelty of war among so-called Christian people.

Burma was not much disturbed by World War I. The first effect on us missionaries was the irregularity of mail delivery. Trains could no longer carry the mail across Europe. There were many delays and gaps in postal service. At long last, I received a letter from Clarence. He had been hurriedly evacuated from Naples on August 4 on the last-to-leave American ship. At Gibraltar, the ship waited four days before daring the Atlantic crossing, and the possibility of German submarines. But now Clarence was home in Massachusetts getting reacquainted with his son, Eastman, now four years old.

Clarence's letters were erratic, giving me only a glimpse of the disturbing situation he faced with the Woman's Board. Its main concern was the care of Morton Lane School. No new recruit had been found to replace me. I would have to remain at the school until they could appoint a new missionary. I never learned all the complications and sessions Clarence went through with Board members until later, especially one unpleasant occasion with the president of the Woman's Board. Letters were so old by the time I read them, he despaired of giving the full information. In the end, Clarence sent me a cable of one word: "Come." But Miss Whitehead could not be left alone at the school. The missionaries decided that if the home Board could not handle our situation, the Reference Committee on the field would have to. And in the end, that is what happened. The committee transferred a woman from her station to the Morton Lane School. The Baptist missionaries in Burma believed all of the mission's work was of equal importance. The missionaries thought it was as essential for Clarence and me to work in Maubin as it was to staff the Morton Lane School.

Clarence's cablegram was really not necessary, for I had no other plan than to leave Burma in November. Neither war nor mission business must interfere with the God-directed turn in our lives. A week before my sailing date (November 10), a serious complication made me hesitate. Turkey had entered the war on the side of Germany. Would the Suez Canal remain open to British ships? Fellow missionaries, the Wiatts, had asked me to take their daughter, Lucy, home to their family. They wanted to put her in school, and were not due for furlough for a long time. I was delighted to have Lucy's companionship, for the thought of a long sea journey, alone among strangers, was not attractive. Now, with the war situation deteriorating daily, Mr. Wiatt said they decided not to send their daughter after all.

"Would you advise me not to go?" I asked.

"No," he said. "If we were all scheduled to go, I would still go. But I cannot ask you to be responsible for Lucy under the circumstances. Your ship may have to sail around Africa."

Another possibility was not even mentioned: that of being taken as prisoners-of-war in Turkey. Neutrals are not always considered friends.

Prior to this, we heard the report of a German ship, the *Emden,* cruising in the Indian Ocean, determined to sink all British ships. The *Emden* became well known because of its captain, a German gentleman who before sinking a ship and its cargo removed all passengers. He took them to some neutral port and left them there, unharmed. German ships raiding at sea were an unpleasant thought, but it was a risk I must face. I had forgotten most of the German I studied in high school, but I still had my German dictionary. That must go in my cabin trunk.

The circle of Moulmein missionaries who had been so pleased and sympathetic with my plans now were divided. Some of them said the dangers were too great. Mrs. Weeks sent me a strong letter of protest, urging me not to travel. "Mr. Chaney would not want you to take these risks." He knew nothing of these "risks" when he cabled, but before he left in June, Clarence had said, "If any serious complication arises, take Mr. Phinney's advice." So I decided to go on as planned and make my final decision in Rangoon.

The Burmese teachers gave me a farewell party held in the kindergarten building where the music teacher taught songs, Bible stories, and a few English words to parents of the day pupils. There were songs and speeches, good wishes, and many tears—some of them my own—but no lasting regrets on my side. The teachers gave me a beautiful gift: a silver cream and sugar set made by a local silversmith. The embossed figures on it shone like white moonlight. I boarded the night train for Rangoon, saying, "I may be back." I would take Mr. Phinney's advice.

In his usual efficient way, Mr. Phinney awaited my arrival at

5:30 a.m., having brought along from the Baptist Mission Press both coolies and a cart for my luggage. After a handshake, he asked at once, "Which trunk for the cabin and which for the hold?"

This took my breath away. "But, Mr. Phinney, do you really think I ought to go with the uncertainty of Suez?"

"Yes, yes," he said, sorting and loading the cart, "go right along. The British ships are well prepared and well controlled. You may have a longer ride, that's all."

"The *Emden*?" I asked.

But Mr. Phinney was already strapping my trunks on the cart. It was plain that the risks of war were minor compared to the urgency of getting me home and married, and back to Maubin.

I boarded a ship of the Henderson Line on November 10, 1914, exactly four years from the day of my arrival. I knew no one on the small passenger list, which included a few women leaving their husbands behind while they went for "extended leave" in England. I soon met a Scottish couple with an adorable baby and became friendly with the only other American on the ship. She had finished a short term as a nurse in the American hospital in Manila. She became interested in my story and my plans. Occasionally we all referred to the *Emden,* and each night I tucked my German dictionary and a small United States flag under my pillow. With these, I would meet the gentleman captain of the *Emden.*

The Indian Ocean in November is a world of beauty and peace. I had brought sewing to keep me occupied. While I embroidered my initials on the huge dinner-sized linen napkins (serviettes to the British), I tried to prepare myself for all possible eventualities. One I could not face was Turkey. A prison? A harem? I put the thought from my mind. I was in God's care and I would trust Him.

The Suez Canal had armed guards posted on both sides. This spoke loudly of the new world of war, though behind the Canal

lay the ancient desert of white sand. Why the authorities let us
pass, we did not know. Later we learned we were the last passenger ship to go through for four years.

What a relief to find ourselves in the Mediterranean! Then
we passed Gibraltar, where Clarence's ship had anchored for a
few days. We continued on to England. I had 24 hours in
Liverpool, enough time to buy a warm coat and a red velvet hat,
surprisingly cheap and good quality. Around the crown of the hat
I placed little white egret plumes I had collected in the rice fields
of Burma. I wore that hat as I disembarked because we heard
rumors that the United States had—or was going to have—laws
prohibiting the import of feathers. With mine in full view of the
inspectors searching my luggage for "contraband," they could
make their decision. I was hiding nothing. I was almost disappointed when the customs officials gave my fine feathers scarcely
a glance.

The usual coastal fogs slowed our approach into New York
harbor, and the landing was delayed until Sunday morning,
December 20. From the rail I saw my sister Edith. She had
brought an up-to-date coat so I could return home properly
dressed. She was puzzled that I had not come home "looking like
a missionary." Many missionaries at the end of a five- to seven-
year term wore the same clothes they wore going out. (I actually did that some years later.) But we found that clothing was apt
to fall to pieces in Burma from the mold and mildew after years
of storage.

What a joy to have Edith beside me as we rode the train to
Rochester. We had four hours to catch up on each other's news.
Father waited at home to receive me. Again we were a family of
three, and I was home for Christmas! Now he not only insisted
on good food for me, but heat as well, lest the December cold in
Rochester give me pneumonia. He stoked the furnace and kept
the rooms so hot that I broke out with prickly heat, something I
never experienced even in the stifling heat of Burma.

The family met in my sister Olive and George Bennett's home for that memorable Christmas. I had interesting, beautiful, and exotic gifts for everyone. Mildred, now 14, attached a glow of excitement to everything related to Aunt Elsie. She sniffed in delight at the musty smell of mildew, saying, "Don't open another trunk till I am here. I just love that Oriental smell!"

Clarence had spoken in my home church when he visited the president of the Woman's Board. It was the custom when missionaries on furlough spoke in the churches that they wore the native costumes of the country where they worked. Burmese men at the time had an unusual, gorgeous way of dressing. When "this man who was going to marry Elsie Northrup" stood before the congregation in a voluminous long silk shirt, a conventional straight loose jacket, and a pink turban of thin silk, they were troubled and could not decide what race he was. Fortunately, Edith set their minds at rest.

Clarence's letters of thanksgiving for my safe arrival were also filled with the joy of spending time with his little son. Grandma Eastman had given over all authority to Daddy. It sometimes bewildered Clarence and left him stranded with indecision. Did he have to spank this boy when he was naughty? How could he?

When Clarence arrived in Rochester, our days were filled with visits to friends and relatives, trying—futilely—to explain the circumstances that had separated us. But we had more important business. Now we could set a date for our marriage in June.

While Clarence continued speaking in the churches of New England, I was giving talks on foreign missions to many church groups and women's circles. It was quite evident that being a missionary meant being available in America whenever needed, whenever invited, and whether or not a church was "mission-minded." Having missionaries speak in church helped to increase prayer and financial support, and interest in the Baptist arm of the missionary work in the Orient. It was our joy to tell the story of the growing church in Burma.

We were married in Calvary Baptist church, on Genesee Street in Rochester, on June 24, 1915. Edith, my maid of honor, was a most helpful sister in all the preparations. Clarence and I would have preferred a quiet, private wedding. But this marriage had a wider significance to the church of which I had been a charter member and to the two Foreign Mission Boards. Now I passed automatically out of the role of spinster missionary under the Woman's Board to that of a missionary wife under the General (Men's) Board. And most of all, our marriage was of interest to the Burma Baptist Mission.

Laura, most logically, was a bridesmaid, and a joyous one— for she was the link who started our friendship. The second bridesmaid was a local girl, a close friend from my church group. Clarence called Eugene, an old friend from Cleveland, Ohio, to be his best man, and two young men from the churches in Irondequoit acted as ushers. The wedding rehearsal included two little children, Rorella and Jimmy. One was to scatter rose petals in front of the bride and the other was to carry (most carefully) the ring. There was a good deal of merriment as Eugene wanted an alternate posted in case someone had to hunt for the ring or wake up the bride to give the proper responses. We were soon in such hilarity that the dear old pastor, Mr. Hutchinson, gently reminded us this was a serious occasion and too much laughter was not appropriate. Later, Clarence commented in some disgust, "Didn't he see that we are not children, and up until now we have made this marriage so serious 'it almost hurt'?" I agreed with Clarence, and for years we laughed together at that old pastor telling us to be serious. But we loved him just the same and had much reason to remember his generosity. He gave us the use of his family's summer cottage on the St. Lawrence River.

On the wedding day, we relaxed. A caterer came to prepare the supper for the wedding party. Edith looked after every detail of my full-length white satin gown and helped Father to look especially handsome. Motor cars were not common then, but Rochester had a taxi service of limousines for those who needed transportation to high-class social events. We ordered a taxi to take Clarence and Eugene to the church, then go to our home for the three of us. But the taxi never showed up. Finally a phone call from the church roused us to some mistake, and one of the ushers said, "I will come for you." It was not a long ride, but a wild one at a speed not usual in the city. It was an open car and Edith was busy catching my long net veil that blew in every direction. I hardly had a chance to adjust dress, train, and veil before I found myself walking down the aisle on Father's arm. I learned afterwards that I was ten minutes late, but I had only a memory of being blown from my home to the altar where Clarence's sweet smile welcomed me and forgave me.

The Hutchinson cottage was a comfortable one on Grinnell Island—one of the Thousand Islands resorts where summer homes of many shapes and sizes were vacation spots for a variety of people from the Vanderbilts of New York City to modest preachers such as Mr. Hutchinson. Clarence and I had the cottage for July and August. A rowboat went with it, and Clarence loved fishing. The easy way was to trail a long towline behind the boat. I could hold that and read aloud to him while he rowed slowly until I reported a catch. I would have nothing to do with the hook and the worms, although I did fry the pike for supper. He did not know until years later that I never eat fish willingly and dislike their smell. By that time I had charitably assumed that he may have disliked some of my pet foods. Fishing in Burma is a commercial occupation, never a sport, so the matter never came up there. Fish gradually disappeared from our diet.

The big event of that summer was the coming of Eastman into our home. At the end of July, Clarence brought him to me. Grandma Eastman, who had loved him back to health and strength, had prepared him for this great event. It always troubled

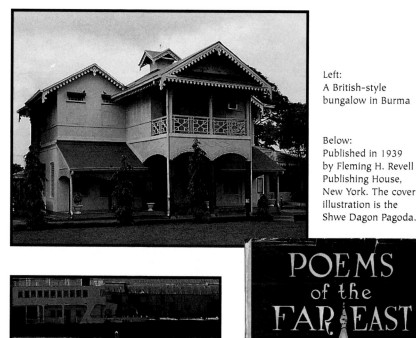

Left:
A British-style
bungalow in Burma

Below:
Published in 1939
by Fleming H. Revell
Publishing House,
New York. The cover
illustration is the
Shwe Dagon Pagoda.

Travel by sampan, especially during
the rainy season

The Northrup Place, ca. 1850

Dr. Clarence Chaney, ca. 1953

Published originally in 1941 by the
Baptist Mission Press in Rangoon

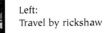

Above:
Clarence and Elsie Chaney,
ca. 1968

Left:
Travel by rickshaw

the little boy that he did not have a mama like his playmates did. So sometimes he called his grandmother "Mama." She always corrected him: "No, I am not your mama. I am your grandma." Now, she told him he was going to have a mama just like other children. He was full of joy and anticipation when Daddy came with the same information. It was a long ride on the train, then by ferryboat to the island. I was preparing supper for them when I suddenly noticed a little boy standing quietly in the open doorway. Thinking him to be another islander, I asked, "And who are you?"

Without any hesitancy or shyness, he answered plainly, "I am Eastman Huggins Chaney."

At that, I dropped my spoon and hurried to him, saying, "You are my little boy!" We were kneeling together joyfully in each others arms when Clarence came in, and with tears in his voice said, "I have waited so long to see this."

We never had a moment of awkward adjustment between us. No memory of our 54 years of married life is sweeter than the joy I had in mothering this lovely child whose heart seemed full of love for everyone. While Clarence and I lingered at the table to talk over his trip, Eastman investigated his new home, running through the rooms upstairs and down. Soon we heard him calling from the front verandah, "Mama, come put me in the hammock." Clarence smiled and said, "I take a back seat now!"

From our first days together, Clarence and I had resolved to keep the custom of "family worship" every morning after breakfast. In the sitting room we knelt for prayer after Scripture reading. Eastman was well acquainted with prayer and with kneeling, as he did at bedtime. Now he knelt at the chair with me, my arm usually around him. Sometimes Daddy's prayers were too long to suit a small boy. I could restrain the wiggling somewhat but not the vigorous repeating of the Lord's Prayer, every word correct and plain, but so fast that once I remonstrated and said, "Eastman, you mustn't say the prayer so fast!" His rejoinder had a touch of pride in it as he said, "Oh, I can say it lots faster than that. Do you want to hear it?" I managed to answer, "No, not now," before he displayed his self-confident prowess in speed of speech.

Back in Rochester, we had a nicely furnished two-bedroom apartment. Mother Eastman came for a two-week visit, and Eastman saw a good chance for relaxed discipline. "Daddy wouldn't dare spank me when Grandma Eastman is here," he said to me confidently. Daddy took the dare, and one day when he deliberately tested this authority, Eastman was spanked. Grandma Eastman was unmoved. Never again was such a scene necessary.

After seeing our medical reports, the Mission Board decided we should stay in the United States until the fall of 1916. That would give me an adequate furlough and would lend Clarence to the intensive deputation schedule speaking on foreign missions that was being set up across the United States. His schedule called for trips of three weeks at a time. It was a great day when Eastman and I would meet his return at the big railroad station and the three of us would have lunch in town. To make the occasion special, Eastman could order anything he pleased. After a long, painful consideration he would invariably choose scrambled eggs, his usual favorite breakfast dish. When it came, he would manfully eat it but mutter to himself, "I'd raver (rather) have Muver's scramble!"

This one trace of his babyhood remained. He had not mastered the sound of "th." In all words that required it, he used the sound "f" or "v." It was his own idea to change my name—Mama to "Muver"—and I loved it. It sounded more grown up than Mama, yet was still a little child's expression. The Burmese word Ma Ma used for all women missionaries in Burma, by old and young alike, sounded exactly like the English word Mama. I was glad for a change from that, and we never tried to correct the "Muver." Eastman and I become great chums. We were seldom separated. When I went to speak to church groups, he begged to go with me. "But what will you do?" I asked. "Well, I could sit and fink," he answered.

Plans for our return to Burma were never far from consideration. Useful articles of all kinds were gradually collected. After one furlough we took back a huge trunk filled with nothing but picture postcards—enough to last five or six years of jungle travel. They were eagerly accepted at the close of a meeting for children on the riverbank who went home waving the cards. Each card had a Bible verse in big black Burmese letters on the back. A card with a picture of Niagara Falls on one side, for instance, would have John 3:16 printed on the back.

One concern related to our return to Burma was of prime importance—Eastman's future. The whole family was opposed to any suggestion of Eastman's going to Burma with us. His mother had died there, and he, himself, as a baby, had almost died. So had Clarence after a severe case of ptomaine poisoning. The Eastman family's opinion of Burma was that it was no place for a white child of any age. They also agreed that Grandma Eastman at the age of 80 was not the one to care for and train a bright, active boy of five. Clarence and I could not bear to be separated from him, but he was nearing school age, and Burma had no American school for missionary children at that time.

Clarence's youngest brother, Roy, a pastor of a small church in Kansas, and his wife, Delia, had no children. They would welcome Eastman. We knew he would have love and care, an education; and they would see that he was never estranged from his father. The war in Europe was still on, and the Suez Canal still closed to traffic, so we planned that in the summer of 1916 we would cross the United States and sail by the Pacific route to Burma. We shared these plans with Eastman, telling him about a new home we would take him to when we had to return to Burma.

He had been so surrounded by love all his life that he had no fears. He and was ready to go to Uncle Roy's if he had to, but the thought of again being without a mother troubled him most. He would come to me at unexpected times saying, "Muver, why do you have to go to Burma?" "Your Daddy's work is there," I said. Or, "They are wanting him to come."

His retort surprised me and left me almost speechless, for he said, "Well, let Daddy go. You stay here with me!"

I knew these were the moments of stress to be met as a missionary. I could only counter by building up Uncle Roy and Aunt Delia, who wanted a "little boy like you," and assuring him repeatedly that we would not forget him and would return to him. Before long he was talking quite naturally about his "new home" in Kansas with Uncle Roy. What a trusting, loving child! One day he left his toys to express what must have been a sudden emotion. He ran to me, his face shining, "Muver! I love everybody in this whole world! And if there is anyone I don't know, I'm ready to love him when I know him!" These treasures of his heart I always shared with Clarence when he came home. Oh, if we could only love like that. This is surely God's way of loving.

Eastman was past five and was to begin kindergarten. It was a great day for him, and for me. I was apprehensive lest it prove unpleasant for this child who had never known any environment other than love and well-mannered playmates. I warned him that in America every boy—bad ones as well as good ones—had to go to school, and if he heard any new words that he did not know, he must ask me before using them. How perfectly he trusted and obeyed me was evident when he came home one day, took me by the hand, and asked in a scared little voice, "Muver, what does 'hist-tory' mean?" I assured him it was "a good word." Each day when he came from school, he paused inside the door to shout "Muver!" When I answered from upstairs, his world was complete. He only wanted the assurance that I was there.

That could not last. We three were on the train headed West in the summer of 1916. When we reached Uncle Roy's home, Eastman took to it immediately. With much delight he ran in and out of all the rooms. He was especially pleased with the special room Aunt Delia had prepared for him. We stayed with him a week, noting how easily and quickly he merged with the family. Soon Uncle Roy and Eastman were real companions. Dreading the final parting, we thought to ease it for him with a gift he had long desired—roller skates. They were hidden till the last morning. While we were closing the suitcases, he was shouting, "Muver, I'm the happiest boy in this whole world!" From our window on the train, through my tears, I saw him doggedly trying to manage the roller skates as we pulled out. I had often heard missionaries say that to leave small children at home was harder on the parents than on the children. I was glad that was true. For all the years Eastman lived with Uncle Roy and Aunt Delia, they gave him love in abundance and more.

As soon as he was able to write a letter, the weekly schedule was rigidly kept between us both ways. I often wondered at the power and patience Roy must have spent to hold that boy to such an unpleasant chore every Sunday afternoon. But what fun the letters were! Despite unheard of spelling, we understood his concern for us and the "muskeetoes." Occasionally, Delia sent us a letter to keep us in touch with his school. "I'm sorry, Elsie, the teacher will not have any 'baby talk' in the first grade. Eastman now says 'Mother' quite plainly."

But I shall always remember the warmth of love that came to me when he said "Muver."

Chapter 8

RETURNING TO BURMA

A dock strike in Portland, Oregon, changed our Pacific sailing to a Japanese line out of Seattle. In August the city was ablaze with flowers, and Clarence began there a favorite last-minute purchase whenever we boarded a ship—flowers for our cabin, to have the good earth with us as long as possible. He loved flowers, but I think this was partly a concession to my poor seamanship. Anyway, it made a pretty snapshot as I walked the gangplank with an arm full of blossoms.

The steamer was one of the neat, comfortable Maru Line, and we lacked for nothing. The little English we heard spoken came from the efficient Captain, who seated me on his left. He tried desperately to entertain me with his own version of the English language. It was rarely intelligible, but I learned it was on the light and funny side and could laugh heartily with him, which encouraged him to practice his English even more to try to please this American missionary.

Like the ships on the Henderson Line going to the East, the Maru Line had a ship going out every two weeks. We had the chance to visit American Baptist missionaries for two weeks in Japan and two weeks in China. Then we boarded the *Inabu Maru* for Singapore. There we had to take our chances on a coastal steamer to Rangoon. It was a slim chance we were told. Had we forgotten there was a war on? We might have to wait 10 days or longer. With that in mind we settled in at the American Methodist Guest House. I called the *dhobbie* to take our dirty clothes from six weeks' travel and lay down for an afternoon siesta. But when I did not know it, Clarence was up and gone. With Burma so nearby, he decided there must be something available. After running around to ship offices, he burst into our room announcing, "I booked passage to Rangoon on a ship leaving this afternoon at 4 p.m." Dirty clothes back in hand, we raced off in a *gharry* to the ship.

If there had been no desperate need because of the war, this small, old British-India coastal steamer would have been scrapped years before. Had we seen where we would have to stay, I doubt we would have had the courage to attempt even a four-day passage on such a ship! The last cabin available was at the rear end of second class over the rudder, and Clarence took it sight unseen. I spent four days of misery, broken only by one heavenly afternoon tea in the cable tea house on a hill in Penang.

When I could sit on deck and listen, Clarence briefed me on my new home and work at Maubin. The Maubin Mission station was the center of a wide area where we would travel to visit churches of the delta and many non-Christian villages during the dry season, just now beginning with the full moon of October.

On arriving in Burma, we spent a few days in Rangoon waiting for instructions, shopping, and attending our Mission conference meeting. How good it was to be back! Even the crows made us feel at home. When all the supplies we needed had been collected, we set off on a day steamer of the Irrawaddy Flotilla Company to Maubin—a ride of six to eight hours, depending on the tides.

The river scenery was another world to me. It appeared a tropical paradise of lush greenery with tiny villages here and there where bamboo houses on stilts housed happy-looking people. I took the delta of the big brown river to my heart. When we passed the Mission compound before reaching the boat landing at Maubin, with great delight Clarence pointed out to me the white launch, the *Harry Morris,* riding at anchor where once the Mission house had stood. The houses of the Mission compound were farther back behind the *bund* (levee) that protected them. They were built of brown teak or bamboo, nestled among tall kokabin trees. The public jetty was a half mile up the river from the Mission. It served the town of 5,000 people with frequent day steamers to many delta towns.

Miss Putnam and Miss Pound were the single women missionaries at Maubin at that time. Miss Putnam was planning to retire soon, but determined first to complete a record of 40 years in one station. She had seen men missionaries come and go. "They seldom stay very long," she said. Later she told how Clarence had endeared himself to the people by staying on at great personal sacrifice when circumstances could so easily have sent him home with the Board's permission. What those lonely years had cost in consecration and resolution no one ever knew.

The mission house for the two women missionaries was spacious. A short, covered runway connected it with the girls dormitory—for all Karen schools, unlike the Burmese, were co-educational.

For the present, the Chaneys would live in the one-room cottage Clarence built from the salvaged timbers of the old house on the riverbank. A corner of the room became our bedroom, another corner our dining room, and a larger space at the front was a combination sitting room, office, and parlor. These divisions were clearly separated by opaque curtains on wires. There was also a narrow front verandah where the tea table was set up each day at 4 p.m. This was all shaded by trees and faced the river. It was livable and pleasant for the few weeks at a time that we lived there. The dry season, which involved evangelistic tours, was upon us, and it was time for us to go into action.

Clarence arrived in Burma for this second term of service as an evangelistic missionary of the delta region with confidence and dreams he did not possess when he first arrived in 1909. He now "was ready to work the field," as he said. He had studied the language of the Pwo Karens to whom he had been assigned, and his preaching and Bible lessons were always done in that language. Pwo Karen was spoken in church services and in most of the Karen homes, but Burmese had become the common delta language and was widely spoken. My Burmese study had not been wasted. I could use it in ordinary conversation everywhere. If the Karen language was to be preserved, it would have to come from the Karen homes and churches. The children did not speak it among themselves and, in time, some of the churches shifted to Burmese.

Clarence and I realized our first terms prepared us for more intensive study and more effective evangelistic efforts. We carefully surveyed the needs of the people and strategized as to how we could make the best of the opportunities. Mission funds designated by the Reference Committee permitted paying the salaries of an ordained preacher named Saya Dee, who traveled with Clarence, and two trained Karen Bible women, Daw Eye Zie and Daw Thein, who would work under my supervision. Both of these women teachers, as they were called, were of great help to the local church women. While Clarence and Saya Dee became reacquainted with the elders of a village, the Bible women and I held children's meetings on the riverbank. The children needed no urging. Our boatman, Thomas, had hardly anchored and put us ashore before they crowded around, ready for any diversion. The teachers set up a big picture roll, told a Bible story, taught one or two Christian songs, and explained about the creator God and why we worshiped him. Mothers hovered in the background. Whether they and the children ever believed the Good News, at least they had heard something they could not easily forget.

While we women taught along the riverbank, Clarence and Saya Dee called at every house, announcing a worship service at noon in the schoolhouse (if there was one) or in the church (if there was one). If the little village had neither, the service was held in a bamboo house or on the riverbank. I played an opening number on the little folding organ while the Christians and their curious friends seated themselves on bamboo mats. This was spiritual worship of a spiritual God, and all came in quiet dignity whether it was Sunday or Wednesday or whatever day Saya Pado (Clarence) could come. After the service everyone sang two or three more hymns, then there was usually a business meeting where problems of the church and village could be discussed and Saya Pado's advice sought. But Clarence never forced any action on the church. The Mission's policy was to establish from the beginning churches that were self-supporting, self-directing, and self-propagating. To do that, the foreign missionary must refrain from any show of authority. We withdrew from a church business meeting after Clarence had given whatever advice he was asked for. Their final vote often proved disappointing to us, but it was their church, not ours.

Along with the women teachers *(sayamas),* I met with the women of the church and made calls at homes where there was some special crisis. Saya Dee made preparations in a nearby non-Christian village for us to hold a meeting in the evening. Again I sat at the little organ on the riverbank while these friendly people came to hear what we had to say. It was all strange and new, but very interesting, and it would be the topic of conversation in the village for the year. Our preaching in the non-Christian villages provided potential understanding of the people in the Christian village who "worshiped a strange God."

In the evening meetings Clarence usually spoke in Karen, using Saya Dee as interpreter for the Burmese. Sometimes when he was tired, he asked Saya Dee to do it all, using Burmese. On one occasion, however, Saya Dee was illustrating the point of God's love by telling the parable of the prodigal son. He used a large illustrated picture roll, and emphasized the eager appeal of the little dog in the picture so much that he almost left out the welcome of the Father. Clarence had to explain that the happy little dog was not the central focus in that story! Dogs in Burma

are half wild, diseased, and not fed and cared for like the one in
the picture. The state of the little dog had evidently registered
with Saya Dee as at least on a par with the Father's forgiveness.

Thanks to the Chaney uncles, we had a lovely, clean cabin in
the *Harry Morris* for a good night's sleep. While Thomas looked
after the engine and the navigation, Clarence and I spent a few
hours of the morning in the cabin getting ready for the next stop
on our tour. This was the pattern of our work during the dry season. Each month between November and April, we spent two to
three weeks visiting the churches and hundreds of non-Christian
villages. Then came the burning hot season, when we spent some
time on vacation, and after that "the rains."

We could not travel during the rains, but problems of the
churches came to us. Elders and deacons found ways to cross
the flooded streams of the delta and ride out the swift currents
in canoes and sampans. The rainy season was also the time for
intensive work at home, in the school, and in town. We wrote
reports and letters, and made friendly contacts with our Maubin
neighbors.

For the farmers, "the rains" meant work season: the time for
plowing and planting rice. Once the ground was prepared, farmers scattered seed. As the little plants shot up, the girls and women
set them out by hand. Usually, the heavens kept them growing in
the humid heat. Then in November came the task of harvesting,
also by hand with sickles, but this was a man's job.

That year, another dream came true. With special funds given
for the purpose, our mission team now had four young semi-
nary-trained preachers working full time for the local churches.
Once a month they traveled to Maubin from the four sections of
the delta, and Clarence spent time discussing the churches they
cared for.

With the Bible women, I worked out a schedule by which
we called on friends of the mission who lived in town. We had
many avenues of friendship among our non-Christian neighbors.

The Bible women were graciously received, especially in homes where the children were regular day students of the mission school. Many of the children also attended the various little Sunday schools we organized in private homes.

As I think about it, I am surprised at all Clarence and I did that first term together at Maubin. "We must have been very young," I find myself saying, then remember we were both well over 30. But we had a backlog of experience to draw on, including much we had learned of the country, of the people, and of the great spread of the gospel all through the land. A *gharry* driver or a rickshaw puller in any accessible town could take you to a well-built American Baptist Mission compound if you said the letters A.B.M. The driver knew nothing of the English alphabet or what the letters stood for, other than it meant a mission compound of decent buildings, a school, a church, and a Christian center where the American missionary lived.

A more powerful engine had been installed in the *Harry Morris,* making it safer when meeting the huge waves of a Mandalay steamer. Thomas, with Clarence's help, had installed it, thereby learning his new profession of river navigation. Thomas still was illiterate but, by special permission of the Rangoon Post Office, Clarence was allowed to interpret and translate the examination Thomas had to pass to secure his livery license to run the engine. This lifted his standing within the community and among the churches about 300%.

During our first touring season, Chinese carpenters imported from Rangoon built the new mission house, well up behind the *bund* this time. Clarence added many extras not found in most mission houses. Maubin's only source of water was the Irrawaddy River, yet every year monsoon rains poured 200 inches on us. In the overhead ceiling of back verandahs, this water was captured from the roof in tanks and piped to the two bathrooms where a faucet opened a thin stream of water into a washbowl. Water for bathing still had to be carried in tins from the river, but we could wash our hands and faces in clean water from the heavens, and pull a plug to empty it down the open drain to the earth below. Clarence added many other conveniences such as cupboards, and closets for hanging damp clothing that could be dried with a charcoal fire. Because of his experience and knowledge of building gained at Northfield, Massachusetts, many years earlier, Clarence was able to stretch the Board's house-building allowance, 4,000 rupees as I remember it (at 300 rupees to the dollar). So airy and comfortable was the new house that it became a display item as I showed guests around. One such guest was Mrs. Cochran, from Pyapan. She exclained with delight as I opened cupboard doors here and there, and called to her husband in the office with Clarence, "Oh, Henry, do see this!" Or, "Henry, have you seen this?" He answered, "Yes, dear, I saw it two months ago—and dreaded the time when you would see it!" I'm sure he heard far too much about the "new Maubin house."

At the same time our house was being built, Clarence oversaw construction of new buildings for the school. A three-story boys' dormitory had been one of Clarence's "dreams" which he now brought into existence. The ground floor contained a dining room and work room. The top two floors were the rooms for sleeping and studying. The compound was large enough to hold several teachers' houses. Their bamboo *bashas* (houses) were scattered all over the property. Clarence developed a football-sized field in the open ground between the school building and the new boys' dormitory. At the back of the field were new teak houses for teachers' families, and the compound took on an orderly appearance.

Clarence also initiated other improvements such as brick walkways between the buildings that solved the mud problem. The little square cottage where we lived while the new house was being built was now available for a new department of the school. It was a surprise to have the government ask us to open a two-year teacher training course to equip rural teachers for jungle schools. This was something the Department of Public Instruction long had in mind. When the director learned that Miss Northrup, who used to write him so many letters from Morton Lane School, was now Mrs. Chaney, he sent an official request to Clarence. He asked if the teacher training program could be established at Maubin since most of the village schools of the delta were Karen. He suggested that Mrs. Chaney, with her education and experience, be appointed as the supervisor of this class, the first of its kind in Burma. If the Department of Public Instruction found it of value to the small village schools, the program would be implemented gradually in all the districts. Clarence and I talked it over and agreed to do it, though we knew it might interfere with some of the touring season. It would be my responsibility, for the course would have to be taught in Burmese. The little empty cottage under the trees was the perfect place for the program. It lay between the house where the two missionary women lived and our new home. So once again I was signing letters, "I have the honour to be your most obedient servant."

The students who took the course were all Karens, but they were at home with Burmese teaching and Burmese textbooks. The real problem was finding a Burmese teacher. The Karens are a clannish people, as are most minority groups, and the Karen elders of the school board were not happy to have a Burmese school on their Karen compound! But the big difficulty came from the teacher himself. He did not have to report to the Karen school board. He did not live on the compound, but spent time there every day. When, after a couple of years, he fell in love with a Karen girl, the place almost blew up.

I was involved in much activity in my first term in Maubin. Many changes were also taking place back home in New York. Edith never failed in writing her weekly letters, but World War I took its toll on mail. Overseas letters arrived on irregular sched-ules and often in such poor shape, mutilated by censors or "salvaged from the sea," that we could hardly read them. Edith and her violin (which had been Father's) had been seated in the Rochester Symphony Orchestra by her teacher, who was also the conductor. She married the cornet player, Fred Roloff. He was appointed as a U.S. Inspector of Immigration, and they made their home in Rouser Point, New York, working the trains in and out of Montreal. Father moved in with Edith and Fred.

At Maubin, Miss Pound went on furlough and Miss Putnam prepared to retire to live with a brother in Mayville, New York. A new single woman missionary was appointed to Maubin in 1918. Clarence had already sent notice to the churches of his coming visit, so I decided to go to Rangoon to meet the new Ma Ma for Maubin. This was my introduction to Carrie Hasseltine, who became like a sister to me.

The Reference Committee decided she should study Burmese instead of Karen, and I was able to help her. Her first responsibility, however, was the care and oversight of the girls' dormitory, on the second floor, level with the mission house where she and Miss Putnam lived. A short covered walk joined the two buildings. Almost at once the Asiatic flu, which was rampant, struck the girls' dormitory. Miss Putnam was quite unable to take on the care of the sick. Only through the resident teachers could Miss Hasseltine talk with the girls, and at one time 30 of them were sick. Yet she did not get it and did not shrink from the situation, new as she was. Her tender love and ceaseless care with the most simple medicines performed wonders. Not one girl was lost. She served at Maubin for many years and returned after World War II to serve in other stations. Few missionaries were so sincerely loved by all races as Miss Hasseltine.

The Asiatic flu was so prevalent that when Clarence and I sat at anchor on our tours in the villages, we often heard the death wail rising from many villages on all sides. Even in this situation the Christians gave witness, for the wailing was not heard in the Christian villages. The grief, I am sure, was no less when a

Christian home was stricken, but the Christians knew that though they grieved their loss, they sorrowed *"not as those who have no hope"* (1 Thessalonians 4:13). Buddhism offers only despair at such a time. What hope or comfort lies in the teaching of endless rebirths into levels of animal, human, or sub-human life if the final end is Nirvana—a state of non-existence?

In times of grief and loss, the Christian faith shines not only in its future hope but also in its immediate good-neighbor policies. One night we anchored at a non-Christian village where only one house was Christian. In that house, parents and children were all ill with the flu. The village elder, a kindly Buddhist man, invited the Bible women to sleep in his house since he did not want them to get the flu. But in the morning, we discovered the Bible women had slept at the sick family's home because the family had "no one there to care for them." The women enjoyed God's special protection, for neither of them got the flu from the family they helped. Nor did Clarence and I get it, though it was all around us.

About a year after the flu epidemic, we found Baby Dot, a pitiful mite of 18 months whose mother had died of flu when the baby was born. A 14-year-old sister held the baby lengthwise, for she was too weak to sit up. Dot was the youngest of seven children. I had met her mother when she brought her twins to our open-air meeting and introduced them as Jacob and Esau. "Isn't that what the Bible says is the name for twins?" she asked when I inquired about their names. Dot had somehow survived under the care of the nursing mothers of the village and her older sisters.

When the day's work was done and the evening meeting on the riverbank of a nearby "heathen village" finished, Clarence and I returned to the *Harry Morris* to sleep. But I could not forget that dying baby. The touring season was nearly ended. Why shouldn't I take that child home and try to restore her to health? Clarence had no objection, but made it clear she was my responsibility. We called the father to the boat and told him I could promise no "cure," but I would try to save his child if he trusted me. We must finish the tour but would be home to receive the baby if he would bring her to Maubin in two weeks.

Three weeks later, I heard a polite cough at the open door of our Maubin home. There stood the father with Baby Dot in his arms. He said, "Ma Ma, here is your baby." I had almost forgotten my promise, but I took the baby at once. A thin muslin dress the father had bought in the Maubin bazaar was all the clothing that came with her.

Clarence was leaving at 8 p.m. by river steamer to help Mr. Conrad at Bassem with the annual refresher class for pastors. Never did I feel so helpless and weak. The father consented to let the 14-year-old sister remain with me for a few days, and with her help I managed to bring life and strength back to the emaciated infant's body, weighing only 10 pounds. In our home she learned to creep, to walk, to laugh, but not to speak. She was a silent child. Clarence and I briefly considered adoption, but put aside the idea as not wise for us. A local pastor and his wife who had no children were eager to adopt her and offered to give Dot a good education, but the father refused and took his baby daughter home. I did not see her again until after furlough, when Dot entered the boarding department of the Maubin school— the only one of her family to be educated up to seventh-grade level. She was not a scholar, but we arranged for her to take a course in home economics, where she learned sanitation and better ways of living. We did not see much of her after that, but she occasionally wrote to us. She was lost in the chaos of the Japanese invasion, and we never knew what became of her. But we never regretted our part in her life.

Burma was not greatly affected by World War I. As a British colony, however, we were conscious of the war in many ways. The young men were keen to enlist in the British Army and some of the bigger Seventh Standard boys of the Maubin School did so. Clarence, as superintendent of the school, had to allow recruiting officers to speak to the boys, and, of course, the older ones were keen to "see the world." When Htin Aung's widowed mother appealed to me to "not let him go," I could only tell her he would return. But when Htin Aung himself begged me to restrain his mother from following him with the Maubin contingent to Rangoon where they eventually sailed for France, I could not do so. I thoroughly sympathized with this son who resented a love that left him humiliated before the others when his mother followed him with unashamed tears to the very gangplank. This was one case with a happy ending, for Htin Aung drove an army truck in Mesopotamia, wrote regularly to his mother, sent money home to her, and returned an upright, sunburned man.

Armistice Day was wildly celebrated even in Maubin, where flags and drums accompanied our little parade, made up mostly of children from the mission school, although Clarence and I walked with them. We had guests visiting from Moulmein at the time. Their two children enjoyed the parade, and all the students were happy, although most of them understood only that there had been a war somewhere and now it was over. We adults who did understand were happiest of all. "There will never be another war," we said. And we believed it. We had "saved the world" for democracy. "There will never be another war!"

THE NOBLE EIGHTFOLD PATH

Right Meditation

Right Mindfulness

Right Effort

Right Livelihood

Right Conduct

Right Speech

Right Intention

Right Views

Chapter 9

GOING ON FURLOUGH

When furlough loomed on the horizon, Clarence and I began referring to it casually and infrequently. But as the time drew near, it became a matter for the Reference Committee and for personal planning. The Mission Board had two methods of providing transportation. They either made ship reservations or gave missionaries the equivalent in cash, allowing them to make their own arrangements.

Clarence enjoyed studying the timetables of various lines. He selected our route, and the mission treasurer in Rangoon made the reservations. In 1922, our first furlough together, we planned to disembark at Port Said, spend two weeks in Palestine, and then sail on the next ship of the Henderson Line. As the time drew near, Dr. J. C. Robbins of the Foreign Mission Board needed a secretary to help prepare his report to the Home Board. He asked the Reference Committee if Clarence and I could sail with him and Mrs. Robbins, so he and Clarence could work on the report during the sea voyage. They were booked on the Bibby Line, a higher class than the Henderson ships. Clarence worked each morning on the upper deck with Dr. Robbins, and they became great friends. Our Palestine trip had to be postponed until our next furlough.

We left the ship at Marseilles, crossing France by land. In 1922, Americans were not well liked there, a fact we felt on every side. Waiters pretended they could not speak English, and we knew no French. Wilson's Peace Treaty of 1918–19 still rankled.

France had endured much and received little. The United States played only a small part in that war, but took a major role in the peace process. We were glad to leave France, but I dreaded the sailing ahead. In the Indian Ocean, I had survived four days of seasickness. I had heard much of the English Channel crossing and was prepared for a rough sea, but it was a quiet and easy one-and-a-half hours of smooth water.

Our route had been planned in relation to Edith's home at Rouses Point, New York, so Clarence and I entered North America via Montreal and proceeded to Rouses Point. We had left only the barest margin of dates that would allow Clarence to attend the alumni reunion of his 1907 class at Yale. It was the one and only time that the five-year intervals of class reunions coincided with furlough.

The 1922 reunion was not as great a joy as Clarence and his old roommate, Bill Taylor, anticipated. Bill and Clarence had shared a room in pre-college days at Mt. Herman, and then again at Yale. They had worked together in business ventures, both of them having to earn their college expenses. Bill was the first of the '07 class to have a child, a son he named Herman Yale. Clarence and Bill and 12-year-old Herman enjoyed a place of distinction at the class banquet. But they found the social and moral tone of some of the diners so distasteful that they, "class baby" in tow, left before the program was over.

While Clarence was in New Haven, I enjoyed Edith's home and the little country village of Rouses Point, where meadows of buttercups and daisies grew in hayfields at the end of the main street. Eastman, now 12, eagerly awaited our arrival in Kansas City where Uncle Roy now pastored the Ivanhoe Congregational church. Thanks to Uncle Roy, Eastman's weekly letters had never failed, but a 12-year-old boy does not disclose much of himself in letters that are a required Sunday afternoon chore. Roy and Delia never usurped the place of Eastman's parents, and we were truly loved and eagerly expected.

When I suggested that Clarence travel alone to bring Eastman home to us, we received strong protest from Aunt Delia, who wrote, "We plan a month together in the Ozarks where the brothers will fish and we will all get reacquainted. Eastman says, 'We can't have any fun without Mother.'" So I joined the party.

The three of us had the use of my father's house on Elliot Street for the school year of 1922–23. Clarence studied at the university and seminary, speaking in nearby churches on the weekends. It was a happy year for all of us. Across the street lived two boys of Eastman's age. They became great friends, and Eastman excelled in school. If I noted a low mark on his report card in one subject, he immediately called my attention to a 90% or higher in some other subject. His attitude toward life and people was one of love, trust, and optimism.

The school year in Rochester ended happily and profitably for Clarence, who passed all oral exams for his Ph.D. After our return to the field, he would write his dissertation on "British Educational Systems in Burma." Eastman was ready to enter high school in September in Kansas City, Missouri.

Our home church, Calvary Baptist on Genesee Street, gave us much love, interest, and friendship. Clarence, by his own decision, changed his membership from New Haven to my church, where he was now well known. During all our years in Burma, we kept our membership in our home church and sent our tithe. This was the mission policy at the time. In this way, we missionaries exerted no voting influence over local churches on the field, since his membership was elsewhere. When our church suggested they divert their entire missionary budget to our work, we declined. We did not want to narrow the church's interest and mission giving to just one field, rather than the wider vision of the need to support Baptist mission work in the other fields of Asia and Africa.

In May 1923, Clarence and Eastman took care of themselves for ten days while I went to Rouses Point to welcome Edith's newborn son, Richard Northrup Roloff, and help care for both of them.

When Clarence and I sailed out of Montreal in 1923, most of my family was present, including my father. Long after the faces blended in the distance, I could see his beautiful white hair. I doubted if I would see him again.

What we did not know as we left the shores of North America was that this was the last time we would see Eastman. Within two years, our 14-year-old son died of spinal meningitis while living with his aunt and uncle in Kansas City. How good God is to withhold the knowledge of future sorrow!

Clarence had worked out our passage allowance in a way that gave us a few days of sightseeing in France and Italy. At Port Said, we connected with the Henderson Line to Rangoon. Then came the long days of shipboard life in which study, writing, and deck games had their due. Clarence was especially good at deck skittles but became almost angry when he found out the other passengers, mostly English colonists, were betting on him! They worked out a compromise which left him free to continue playing. He also enjoyed the game of deck bowling with an almost inner sense of the alley's slope as the ship rolled.

One morning we wakened to a strange odor in the sea air. As we neared the coastal waters of Burma, Clarence and I recognized the essence of mold and mildew that appears at the end of the rains. Soon we drifted in the coastal waters of Burma's many rivers with seagulls overhead welcoming us. Although conditions often made it necessary to shift missionary personnel, to our delight there was no such complication in October 1923, and we were posted back in our home in Maubin along the wide, swift, brown Irrawaddy River.

In our absence, the four young evangelists had kept wise oversight of the local churches. One of Clarence's first activities with them was an all-day debriefing session. Their reports revealed one or two trouble spots and one openly divided congregation, the only problem of that kind we ever saw. Clarence made a personal visit to that church and village, where he helped both parties reconcile on the basis of Christian witness to their non-Christian neighbors. This brought a response of repentance and brotherly love. The division was healed and Christian harmony restored. All was forgiven; all were happy; and we never heard the quarrel referred to again.

Thomas and the *Harry Morris,* evangelist Saya Dee, and the Bible women joined Clarence and me once again. But the old, easy tolerance of the Buddhist people had changed. No longer could Westerners in leather boots and shoes tread casually on "sacred ground." Shoes and socks must be removed before walking around on the open terrace of the Shwe Dagon Pagoda or even climbing the long flight of stairs from the street level.

A new spirit of self-determination permeated the country. A new vocabulary was heard at the university, including terms such as boycott, non-cooperation, and anti-British government.

The Prince of Wales was scheduled to make an official visit to Rangoon. How could people ask their future king to bare his feet? The Shwe Dagon Pagoda trustees were almost in tears from embarrassment. Even the King of Siam (now Thailand) rebelled against this regulation. He flatly refused to remove his military boots, saying the Siamese (now called Thai) people were just as good Buddhists as the Burmese, and never required "foot-wearing" to be removed.

After days of indecision, the Shwe Dagon Pagoda trustees decided to make a rare exception for their future king. When the matter was brought before the Prince of Wales, he delayed answering, then politely refused to visit the Golden Pagoda. He said he would not tread where the humblest or richest of his subjects could not go in usual dress. In spite of the anti-British feeling in the university, the state affairs for the Prince's visit were followed without incident. In a special gathering of the Karens, a quartet of male voices made such a "hit" with the young prince that he called for encores. Ever after, these four Karen men sang together, even in their old age, and were officially booked on many state occasions as "The Prince of Wales Quartet."

But the new post-war spirit became more evident. No longer did the youth in the movie houses stand for "God Save the King," and many purposely walked out with a clatter while it was being played. "Home Rule" was the talk of the day, though few people knew or could explain what it meant.

Clarence and I were attending our Annual Missionary Conference in Rangoon when university students began a boycott in which Judson College joined. We were shocked to hear that Christian boys were demonstrating, lying full-length across the thresholds of the classrooms. No one could enter, for it was unthinkable that anyone would step across a prostrate student. Such behavior would be so uncivilized as to make the offender sub-human. The students' demonstrations meant there could be no term examinations, and the university closed.

The wave of political disturbance increased. The government was slow to take action, but when U Ottama, a well-educated Buddhist priest, spoke openly in the parks of the shame and injustice of a foreign government "exploiting the wealth of Burma," he was arrested for sedition and put in jail. He was tried in the little courthouse at Maubin because of the danger of riots in Rangoon. I happened to be in town that morning and saw him led under guard from prison to the courthouse, a distance of two blocks. About 20 Burmese women knelt beside the road. As he approached, they put their foreheads to the earth and flung their long black hair over the path so that he might walk on it.

In Rangoon, it was mostly young men who expressed rebellion. A most regrettable incident occurred when a young American couple, newly arrived for missionary service, was attacked on the street by seven young priests who had been stirred to action after a political speech. With long knives (daos) they went out to kill the first Englishman they saw. Not able to tell the difference between the English and Americans, the priests badly cut the Gleasons, who had only an umbrella for self-defense. Fortunately, they were near a hospital and received excellent medical care. They refused all compensation they were entitled to in the courts.

The result of this incident was a wave of shock and horror from the whole Buddhist community. Even in our little river town, Buddhist friends and some Buddhist priests we had never met before called on the mission and told us their shame that missionaries in their land had been so unjustly treated. The spokesman continued, "Everyone knows that missionaries are here to help the people, not to oppress them like the British government."

Clarence and I did not stay in Maubin very long after our return in 1923. The Reference Committee needed someone to fill the Field Secretary position in Rangoon while Dr. Wiatt took furlough. By general consent and by the annual vote of the missionaries, Clarence became Acting Field Secretary in 1924. Miss Bonney, the efficient secretary, was transferred to a frontier station.

The Rangoon office was responsible for local matters, as well as serving the 140 American Baptist missionaries located in 42 stations throughout Burma. Many departments of the Mission's ministries were located within Rangoon. These included churches catering to a variety of ethnic groups, Judson College, City Mission Society, Baptist Mission Printing Press, and the Mission Guest House.

Clarence came and went to Rangoon while I stayed in Maubin for a few months. Once or twice I attempted to answer a call from one of the jungle churches. With the Bible women and the *Harry Morris,* travel was easy. While I could not and did not attempt to give the advice, encouragement, and inspiration that Clarence did, I could at least listen and report the needs of the churches to Clarence. One time while traveling by river steamer to Maubin, smoldering fire broke out in the hold. Before I knew it, the steamer turned toward shore and passengers scrambled to the bank in three feet of water. I hesitated, though smoke was pouring from the hold. An elderly Burmese gentleman saw my predicament and carried me piggy-back to the shore.

Clarence and I spent Christmas in Maubin, making it lively for the school children and unloading from our trunks most of the gifts and treasures we had stored for the years ahead. The most special was the parade of 200 celluloid dolls purchased at 10 cents each from Woolworth's. The Women's Society of my Rochester church had daintily dressed each of the three-inch dolls, even to little picture hats. We gave these to the children of the six little Sunday schools in Maubin. For years, local Christians faithfully carried on these meetings every Sunday morning. The Buddhist parents had cooperated, saying, "All the stories and songs are good words for children to learn."

But now the revolt against a "foreign government" meant new attitudes toward all foreigners. Our position in the country as American missionaries was not quite as secure as before, and one time when I stayed alone in Maubin there were threats to burn the Mission. Friends warned me of this possibility. It was a long, dark night as I kept guard, relying on several Karen men to cover the compound and strike the hours all night on a gong so neighbors would know we were alert. Fortunately, nothing happened, and by the time I joined Clarence in Rangoon, Miss Putnam and Miss Hasseltine were not at all troubled to continue living in Maubin.

The active opposition to foreign government died down while various groups of Burmese and Karens on home-rule committees traveled back and forth to round-table discussions in London, England. Sydney Loo Nee, acknowledged leader of the Karen delegation, appeared at the Governor's Annual Garden Party in formal dress, complete with silk hat, striped trousers, and white spats. Sydney Loo Nee came often to the Field Secretary's office to talk with Clarence, for he was an outstanding Christian, whether in Burma or in London.

With the closing of schools in March and the hot weather vacation, followed by the May monsoon rains, it seemed that Clarence and I should both settle in at the Field Secretary home in Rangoon. The needs of the office could best be served from Rangoon. The office also needed a resident wife who was called upon in various ways to act as hostess and helper. We did as little moving as necessary, expecting to return to Maubin in November when the Wiatts returned. But before the rains ended, word came that Dr. Wiatt's health made it impossible for him to resume the work of Field Secretary. If he were able even to return to Burma, it must be to some other work. The vote of the Missionary Conference made Clarence Field Secretary. The missionaries extended this by annual ballot for 13 years.

Chapter 10

LIVING IN RANGOON

Before the end of 1924, we had moved our belongings to the upper floor of the house at 121 Mission Road, Rangoon. The Mission compound, with many buildings on a 12-acre lot, had its own well. The water carrier *(pani-wallah)* used the well to water plants, but bath water came from the hydrants. We still used the boiling and filtering process for all drinking water. After a half-crazed Indian jumped into the well one afternoon, we discontinued all contact with the well for three days while a good dose of potassium permanganate disinfected it. Later, the same man returned and repeated his method of cooling off on a hot day. After that, we closed the shallow well.

If I had expected Rangoon to be free of mosquitoes, I was disappointed. There were plenty, and Clarence and I were driven to all sorts of methods of protection: mosquito nets on the bed, of course; citronella oil to smear on legs and arms; and joss sticks burning in little bowls under the table. A gracious hostess gave a pillow slip to dinner guests at the table. Hemlines went up after World War I, and the mosquitoes took advantage.

But after living in Maubin where mosquitoes worked both day and night shifts, Clarence and I could endure the mosquitoes. Foreign visitors thought it an exaggeration when they heard that farmers in Maubin district kept their oxen under nets at night. But Clarence and I had seen this often. The cattle pens had mud-covered bamboo walls three-feet high. Above that, hung the mosquito nets of cheap muslin to protect the cattle and conserve their strength for plowing by day.

I once sat at dinner in Miss Putnam's house in Maubin when two American members of the Woman's Board were visiting. One asked Miss Putnam how long she had lived there. When Miss Putnam replied, "It will soon be 40 years," Mrs. B. gave a vicious slap at her own arm and said wearily, "I hope you will have many stars in your crown in heaven!"

The strange thing about the pesky mosquitoes in the Maubin area was that the one malaria-breeding variety—the anopheles—was not found there. One time in Maubin I was ill and called the doctor who, finding that I had malaria, asked, "Where have you been?" Clarence and I had been to the Kachin Hills on vacation. A strenuous program of quinine for three weeks provided the cure, and I never had malaria again.

In Rangoon, I found the ants a greater trial than the mosquitoes. And, although not as common, the occasional visitation of snakes proved even more disturbing. How two snakes could appear near midnight in the shallow-rimmed bathing area of our bathroom can only be explained by a guess—that they had crawled up the open drainpipe from the ground at least 20 feet below. But our wildest guess could not explain why, in opening the closed house for our return after a two-week absence, we found a snake neatly coiled on a dining room chair, appearing completely at home.

During our 13 years in Rangoon I made many trips with Clarence to the far frontier stations. But when he responded to calls for help from nearby mission stations that could be reached by train or boat, I found many avenues for service close at hand, and remained in Rangoon. After the office secretary, Miss Bonney, moved to a distant Kachin station, Clarence had an Indian man, S. O. Daniel, as his secretary. I took no part in Clarence's official life other than taking on certain responsibilities at the request of the Reference Committee. Rarely did Clarence "talk shop," and I never brought up mission problems, for I well knew his need for relaxation in the few hours we had together.

I was amused one day when a woman asked me for information concerning a rumor. I answered simply and truthfully, "I have not heard anything about it." She wouldn't believe me and said, "You are the Field Secretary's wife. You should know everything that goes on in the mission!" I disagreed with her heartily, and finally she left, disappointed. But I was glad the troublesome matter had never been mentioned to me.

As hostess in the beautiful and spacious upstairs apartment, I was grateful for the dependable household helpers (called "servants" in that era) who worked with me. All our servants were Indian. The Burmese had never been trained for such work and would not "stoop" to serve a white man. In a few rich Burmese homes, I saw Burmese servants—elderly retainers, poor relations, or friends—who needed a home and performed services in exchange for room and board.

All the time I was in Rangoon, I had a good cook named Anthony, a Roman Catholic with a sweet wife and two children. American guests were surprised to be served delicious, hot gingerbread, and even more surprised when I told them it was baked over an open charcoal fire under a kerosene oil tin with coals on top. I never owned an American stove in Burma, nor did I ever see one.

A covered walkway connected the cook-house with the dining room. Along the wall stood a sink and drainpipe for washing dishes. The washing-up was done by the "bearer," a young man who served food at the table, washed dishes, made beds, and dropped the mosquito nets over them in the evening, tucking them carefully under the mattress and leaving only one small spot loose for entrance. In Maubin, Clarence often took a candle and matches inside because it was impossible to enter the net, however quickly, without a few mosquitoes coming to bed with us. I never dared that trick, but Clarence could hold the little flame under the insect to scorch its wings without accident to the net.

It was understood that the master of the house *(sahib)* and his wife *(memsahib)* were morally responsible for the care and well-being of their servant and his family. In times of sickness, in crises of debt, or when the wife needed a sewing machine so she could make the children's clothing, Ma Ma was called on to help finance this by withholding five rupees per month from Anthony's wages till the machine was paid for. And when the next baby was expected, the family expenses increased.

The *pani-wallah* (water carrier) was a Muslim who did not know any English. His routine was to carry water to the kitchen and to the bathrooms. He poured the water in big jars, which we emptied over our heads and bodies. This was called a "pour bath." He also watered the clay pots of brightly colored flowers that lined our driveway and the ferns on our covered front verandah.

I had little contact with the *pani-wallah* other than to hand him his monthly salary, receive his courteous greeting, *"Salaam"* (peace be on you), and marvel at his strength. I watched him climb the stairs to the cook house or to the bathroom with the heavy two-gallon tins of water hanging from his shoulder yoke. He was a small man, loyal and faithful in his work until he was imprisoned on a charge of debt. This, he said later, was a frame-up by two unscrupulous friends. Six months of idleness (by English law, only criminals must work in prison) with regular food and no tobacco or betel nut allowed, brought him back to work looking fat and happy. We never did learn the whole story, but it must have been very complicated since, in accordance with British law, the accusers paid his board for six months.

One other servant, more necessary than the rest, was the sweeper who came every morning to sweep the floors with his broom made of long sticks and dried palm leaves. Once a week he swept the cobwebs off the ceiling with a 15-foot-long broom, and once a week he washed all the floors with plain water. This routine, along with the daily tread of bare feet, polished the teak floors so nicely that I never wished to cover them with rugs. The sweeper, younger than the other staff members, was a Christian named Matthew. He wore khaki shorts and a white shirt, but he was always freshly bathed, with his hair oiled and combed. In spite of his low-caste work, he was liked by all the servants in our house and in the Mission Guest House next door, where he also worked. To see his unfailing charity of spirit among the non-Christian servants, in whose house or room he must not step, was an outstanding testimony of Christian joy and peace.

Because Rangoon had no sewer system at that time, twice a day Matthew climbed the back stairs to the bathrooms to carry out the commode pots in a covered basket. They were returned empty, washed and as clean as Matthew himself. I often wondered if a similar service was carried out in the governor's mansion less than two blocks away.

When Dr. Wiatt was the Field Secretary, an American guest observed how his host was hampered by having to depend on *gharries* for transport, and gave a Ford car to the mission. Cars were not common in Burma then, but Dr. Wiatt found the car so convenient and time saving that he showed Clarence how to use it. Clarence insisted I, too, learn to drive. I was terrified at the thought and resisted until Clarence appealed on the grounds of the help I could provide to him and the mission by meeting him at the train and boat. I was not as familiar with engines as he was, and he had little patience with my hesitancy and fears. Nevertheless, I did learn to drive the "Tin Lizzie," and used it more or less happily in the streets of Rangoon, where my hand most often hovered on the bulb of the horn to warn pedestrians, carts, *gharries,* cows, bicycles, and coolies to get out of the way.

I found more avenues for missionary service than I could fill. At the request of the Reference Committee, I became Superintendent of the Mission Guest House. This spacious, two-story building was more like a small hotel for 20. The two family rooms boasted cots and trundle beds for young children. As manager of this facility, used by out-of-town missionaries and many other guests, I had entire charge of the staff, accounts, reservations, correspondence, and all equipment and furnishings (and their repairs). To see that the rooms were cleaned and ready for occupants, the laundry cared for, all the food fresh and free of ants, and to at least try to keep the rooms and bureau drawers free from cockroaches would have been impossible with less responsible servants.

I also had the care of the servants' quarters, suitable wooden houses at the back. The stigma of "outcaste" would never be noticed or recognized in an assembly of Christians, but Matthew's own little house had to be kept separate from the others. That did not prevent the servants from becoming friends. It was one of them who told me Matthew's house was "falling down." So it was. The house funds being adequate at the time, I called the Chinese carpenter. The result of his work was a new little house. One day when Matthew and I were talking, he suddenly asked, "How much money Ma Ma getting for Ma Ma work?" I could never make him understand that I received no pay. No missionary wife ever did, though most of the wives took on regular duties, sometimes teaching English classes, training choirs, and organizing Sunday schools.

Matthew and his wife liked their new house. But trouble arose between them. One day I faced them on a side verandah to hear a grievance previously unknown to me. For some reason, they were living apart. In her long loose sari the wife looked like a child, though she was obviously pregnant. Matthew had evidently agreed to a session with *Memsahib,* but he was adamant in his refusal when I asked him to forgive his wife. I could only suspect he had "loaned" her to another man because the couple had waited so long—in vain—for a child. She complained bitterly that Matthew refused to care for her. Matthew reiterated that he would not take his wife back "until God has blessed us." I was utterly nonplussed, and sent them away with a word of prayer. A few months later, a baby son was born. There was nothing but joy and smiles all through the servants' quarters. When I asked Matthew his baby's name, he said proudly, "Solomon." He referred to the child as "Ma Ma's baby" when he spoke of him. I took more comfort, however, from the fact that Solomon certainly looked like Matthew. Often when Matthew worked in our house, I inquired about the baby's health.

All seemed well until one afternoon when Matthew called and said, "Ma Ma's baby is sick." I found Solomon having convulsions. All the servants and their wives gathered in concern outside the quarters. I knew how serious convulsions could be! This long-hoped-for baby must not die. Quickly I directed various ones to gather a tin bathtub and two tins of water. We all had to wait in prayer while the water heated. I held Solomon submerged in the warm bath and gently rubbed his back while his parents held his head above water. Little by little, the baby relaxed. When all signs of convulsions passed, he lay sleeping in his mother's arms. We had a prayer of thanksgiving. I expect I was the only one who noticed how the separation of caste faded. At that moment, the staff were all Matthew's friends. They, too, were fathers and mothers. And Solomon lived.

In Rangoon, each individual missionary and couple was assigned to an ethnic group. A few worked in English, and if we, who had to sweat over the "impossible" foreign words and sounds of Burmese or Karen or Kachin, were inclined to envy them, a short time in the city cured us. The missionaries who taught at Judson College and the American missionary pastor of Immanuel Baptist church had their problems, too.

This city church was primarily for Anglo Indians and Anglo Burmans, but it became an integrated congregation for any who wanted to worship in the English language. Burmese, Tribals, Chinese, and Armenians attended. We used the word "church" in its New Testament meaning—a group of believers, not a building. Immanuel Baptist Church's history began with the early British occupation of the country when some in the British army were nonconformists. The church ministered through many years and owned a splendid building in the heart of Rangoon. Clarence and I usually attended the worship service every Sunday evening. We came out into the afterglow of sunset and felt a benediction to the day which began for me at 8 a.m., when I taught a class of girls at the Sunday school hour. Between the two English services at 8 a.m. and 6 p.m., Indians speaking Telagu or Tamil, Karens, and a small group of Chinese held services in the building.

Clarence often preached at the church. He also enjoyed speaking at the Pwo Karen Chapel on our Mission Road compound. On the same tract of mission land, the large Sgaw Karen school building hosted a neighborhood church.

In December 1937, we received the amazing news of the abdication of England's King Edward VIII. The press confirmed it the next morning, and his farewell speech to the Empire was made public. The woman for whom he had renounced the throne was Wallis Simpson, an American divorcée, and Clarence and I could not hope to be spared entirely from the taint of the situation. But with their typical reserve, the British took the news in calm silence. I never heard the matter mentioned even by our closest friends. The King was dishonorably "dead." Long live the new King!

My neighbor, a lonely, old British woman whom I often called on, needed me now more than ever, although I dreaded visiting her after this news. I found her greatly changed by the terrible blow to one who had worked so long and hard for the British Empire and, as Clarence sometimes said, confused it with the Kingdom of God. Her patriotic enthusiasm was humbled. We tried to talk of other things, but some word had to be spoken, and I was not the one to do it. This one time, and never again, she spoke of the subject that burned between us. She asked, "What do you think about this situation?"

I could say nothing to ease her mind and was startled by her remark. "Someone must have put something in the drinks they have at their parties!" This thought grew out of her childhood in India, where the servants' gossip included talk of "love potions." This was worse than the actual facts, I thought, but perhaps it eased her disappointment. My neighbor never rallied to her old spirit and, as the hot season approached, she quietly slipped away from us all.

It fell to me to work with young women from the Salvation Army in emptying the old house, which she willed to the Salvation Army. We worked for days, listing page after page of books, china, clothing, and much more. Streams of perspiration poured onto our notepads.

That year, the American Baptist Mission Conference held its meeting in cool Taunggyi. Clarence had gone ahead, and I joined him after completing my work in the old house. That neighbor was my last living link with the 1880's. She was gone, but she had greatly enriched my life.

Clarence and I turned our thoughts toward our last actual furlough. When we returned to the United States at the end of the next five-year term, we would retire. But to where? We had never seen California, a place many friends recommended to people like us who had spent our lives in the tropics. We decided to sail via the Pacific and investigate California. While these plans were under way, Clarence had another decision to make. He had served two complete terms plus an extra year in the Rangoon office and had decided a younger man should serve as Foreign Secretary. He realized he was very tired and, at times, unwell. Could we not spend our last term of service in a mission station working for a localized ministry? With that in mind, Clarence presented his resignation from the post of Foreign Secretary at the October Conference in 1937.

Each of us went about our tasks, conscious that someone else soon would take over. Following the Mission Conference, Clarence attended all the mission committees, patiently helping each one in its decisions. Then came a period of packing and disposing of personal furniture, knowing that when we returned for our final term, Clarence and I would live in some other place. We were saying "goodbye," not just to the office and our work, but also to the comfortable house we had enjoyed for 13 years.

Clarence and I took a ship to Singapore, finding among the passengers an American couple who reminded us it was Thanksgiving Day in the United States. They invited us to join them for the special dinner they ordered; otherwise, I doubt if Clarence and I would have noticed the holiday, since every day seemed like Thanksgiving Day to us. We gave thanks for the six years of worthwhile work accomplished; thanks for God's care over us and all the circumstances we had lived through; thanks for the farewell speeches of deep appreciation given by local groups and the Karens; thanks for the upcoming furlough which we both needed; thanks to God who had allowed each of us to be a missionary.

At some port, our ship took on tons of shredded coconut being exported to the United States to manufacture soap. The holds had to be left open because of heat. We not only saw the coconut, but the sweet smell became nauseating as we trailed the perfume across the Pacific Ocean. We spent Christmas Day in port in Hong Kong. As Clarence and I climbed the hill to a church and found ourselves just in time for the Christmas service, we thanked our Norwegian sailors for this blessing.

By appointment, we met cousins from Leonia, New Jersey, in Manila. Their son, Wilmot DeGraff, taught in the Brent School at Baguio, and his parents were visiting him. Clarence and I spent our day on shore with them—sightseeing, eating lunch, and enjoying a long afternoon in a seaside park where we closed the day watching a marvelous crimson, gold, and rose-colored sunset through the coconut palm–lined shore.

With Christmas Day and Manila behind us, the *Pleasantville* made a straight crossing to San Pedro. There was nothing to stop us, not even the International Date Line where we doubled a Tuesday. Did that even up with the Sunday we had dropped in 1916 going West?

This voyage gave Clarence and me rich memories of our first voyage across the Pacific in 1916. That time we had sailed far to the north. This was another ocean to us, mild and warm—and sometimes when the wind blew our way, fragrant. On this sea journey we endured one short storm, which I spent in my usual manner: seasick in the cabin. Clarence, of course, enjoyed every minute of it on deck. Fortunately, he missed the huge wave that crashed against the bridge and destroyed part of the structure. Those who know the ways of ships better than we do said this destruction was a great embarrassment to any experienced sea captain, which explains why we entered the harbor after dark.

The Mission Board's West Coast representative met Clarence and me when we landed. He presented Clarence with a request from Board headquarters in New York, asking him to interview a man who lived in San Diego the next morning. This philanthropist wanted information about a new building at the Insein Seminary for which he planned to pay the entire cost. The trip to San Diego took our whole first day in California, but the gift was assured. Little did we think then that when we returned to Burma we would work in that new building.

With the help of friends, Charles and Mabel Weeber, Clarence and I secured a comfortable apartment in Los Angeles, where we spent the winter while considering California as the place for our retirement.

The mysteries and surprises of a grocery store in January 1939 were baffling. When I asked for milk, I faced a battery of questions: "What kind of milk?"—and a half-dozen varieties were named. I was relieved to learn they all related to cow's milk, not goat's or buffalo's. The same thing happened when I asked for bread. A dozen and more kinds sat on the shelf. Shopping was a slow, bewildering business. How had the United States changed so in seven years?

With Charles' help and experience, Clarence began shopping for a used car we could drive to Rochester. In the end, Clarence decided to accept the Weebers' offer of a seven-passenger Packard they had used little and stored carefully for five years. The Packard used more gas than a smaller car, but if we didn't have to buy a car, it would not cost more in the end. We would use it only a year. We both passed our driver's tests, named the Packard "Sir Charles" after its donor, put our luggage in the back, and headed East. We drove in a zigzag route, keeping Sunday appointments and visiting family all along the way.

We had no fixed home during that furlough. Our "headquarters" was in Rochester at my sisters' homes. But to avoid the Upstate New York winter of 1938–39, we became guests of Mrs. Doane in the Houses of Fellowship at Ventnor, New Jersey. This group of houses, built and sustained by Mrs. Doane, was open to all missionaries on furlough, rent free. The compound housed 200 people when all apartments were filled. Missionaries were received with the status of "guests of Mrs. Doane." Each apartment, fitted to the size of families or singles, was completely furnished. If residents gave notice of their arrival, they found food for the first breakfast in the icebox. At Christmas, Mrs. Doane supplied a turkey for each apartment. She asked only one thing of the residents: the guests should conduct a mid-week devotional meeting, at which time only her father's (William H. Doane) hymns would be sung. This was no hardship, since they were well-known and much-loved hymns such as "To God Be The Glory," "Near The Cross," and "Rescue The Perishing."

Clarence traveled for most of our furlough. His itinerary took him anywhere east of the Rockies. Surrounded by so many missionary friends, I never felt lonely. Frequent train service ran out of Ventnor to New York City and beyond. I tried a surprise visit to my sister in Rochester, arrived on a late train, and found the city buried in deep snow. With much difficulty, the taxi driver managed to reach the house and left me there at 11 p.m., desperately trying to waken the family. My only shelter was an enclosed back porch. Fortunately, I did not have to spend the rest of the night there.

There were few Baptist churches in the vicinity, but I began receiving requests to address women's clubs and groups for women where the usual missionary talk was neither wanted nor understood, but I found a way to interest these women. From the many poems I had written, giving the atmosphere of Burma, I selected a few to combine with lecture material on the people, the religion, and the beauty of the country. Half of the lecture was explanatory and descriptive, and half was reading my own verse. I did this fearfully at first, hoping to learn whether my writing had any real value. It was so well received that I frequently heard the question, "Why don't you have your poems published?" Encouraged by words of appreciation, and by letters and telegrams from Clarence, I prepared a manuscript of my verses. One day in New York, I walked into the Fleming H. Revell Publishing House with my manuscript. *Poems of the Far East* was published and went on sale just two weeks before Clarence and I sailed.

The more than 54 years of our marriage left me with countless dear memories of Clarence's unfailing love, but I think none touched me more than his suggestion that on our return trip to Burma we use land travel as much as possible. This was to compensate me for the many unhappy days of seasickness I had endured. I accepted the plan with joy, despite knowing it would mean much extra work for Clarence in preparing routes and timetables.

The DeGraff cousins sent us off aboard the S.S. *Exochordia* on April 22, 1939. Every day at breakfast, Sparks (the nautical nick-

name for radio operators) gave us a news sheet. Every day an
English woman casually asked as she took her seat at breakfast,
"Has war been declared yet?" Her husband worked in the oil
wells in Syria. She told me she considered an American ship safer
than a British one at this time.

Even with the threat of war looming in the background, we
enjoyed many unique and enriching experiences in this hop-
and-skip journey across two continents. Clarence and I found
much suitable background material for teaching at the Divinity
School, even though at the time we traveled through Bible lands,
we did not know we would be teaching. Having for so many
years lived with the Bible, it was a great moment when, with our
own hands at the old site of Babylon, we picked up large, sun-
dried bricks bearing the mark of King Nebuchadnezzar. Any
class we later taught about old Roman and Greek pre-Christian
days heard us tell of the enormous temple ruins at Baalbeck. We
had an incredible bus ride by night from Damascus across the
bare desert, with no roads and only a post and a sign on a limit-
less horizon telling the driver he was on the right "road" to
Baghdad.

When we caught the plane at Calcutta's Dum-Dum airport,
we saw black monsoon clouds ahead. This was our first plane
ride, and though we had a bit of turbulence, we were soon flying over the checkerboard of green rice fields, the Delta River,
and—oh, joy!—the Rangoon airport. It had been a three-hour
ride instead of a three-day boat trip. We arrived in Burma for our
last term on June 6, 1939.

Despite having such short notice from Calcutta of our arrival, 19 missionary friends met us at the airport to see our plane
land. I think the younger missionaries were proud that the
Chaneys (the "Baptist Bishop," as they called Clarence) were the
first to break the old pattern of sea travel. The Rangoon Airport
is ten miles from the city, but only one mile from Seminary Hill
in Insein, where our friends, the Wiatts, lived. Clarence and I

went home with them so we could talk over the question that had hung in our minds—where would we live and serve this last term?

The Foreign Service office and the Reference Committee had made our assignment, awaiting Clarence's approval and acceptance. Dr. and Mrs. Wiatt would retire at the end of this school year. The new building of the Divinity School, the funding of which Clarence had secured from the philanthropist in San Diego, was in full use. The mission asked us to begin work in the Baptist Divinity School, and the following March when the Wiatts left, Clarence would become its president.

Chapter 11

CHANGING RESPONSIBILITIES AND
MENACING REALITIES

The Karen Theological Seminary had been training and sending preachers and pastors to the Karen churches for almost 100 years. Along the crest of the same ridge of land, the Burmese Seminary served the Burmese churches. But the time had come when young men of college age, educated mostly in English, were ready to give their services to Christian work. They needed a larger source of library material than was available in either Karen or Burmese libraries. They were able to preach in either language, perhaps both in the same service, because they were all bilingual. The college-level Divinity School had been organized in 1927 to provide a higher level of education for them. It graduated its first class under Dr. Wiatt's leadership, and now had an enrollment of 20 students of many races.

To live on "Seminary Hill," as the lovely tree-shaded compound was called, to work with these fine young people, and to teach classes in our own language—what a boon for our final term. A spacious, two-story teak house awaited us next door to the Wiatts. Clarence and I soon settled in this comfortable home.

Clarence was at work again, studying long hours at his desk and teaching classes in the subject he loved best—his friend of a lifetime, the Bible. I took over classes Mrs. Wiatt taught: English literature, hygiene, and a smattering of the elementary sciences. Although the students had taken some college courses, English was still a foreign language and they needed coaching in its usage.

With the aid of a little Fiat, Clarence and I could reach Rangoon easily for errands and meetings. On Sundays, Clarence often preached at the English services for the Anglo-Indians in Rangoon, or at the seminary in Insein, or at Judson College. Sometimes he preached in Karen to the church at the Pwo Karen Bible School, which continued at its old site on Mission Road.

Although I had been away from my teaching profession for awhile, I found the associations of a classroom—even though on a college level—familiar and pleasant. The blackboards, the smell of chalk, the papers, and the explanations revived the atmosphere of a school where students were eager to learn and a teacher was respected. These students were not children, and I had to remember that. Three of them were married; one was a teacher in the Karen Seminary attending the Divinity School to "better understand English." One was a Presbyterian preacher from Thailand; another a Methodist from China. Two were leaders from the Naga tribe in Assam. One was Indian, four were Burmese, and the others were all Karens. The only common language in a school such as this was English, and it was the only Divinity School of its level between Serampore (in Bengal, India) and Singapore at that time.

From my study upstairs I could hear the men singing the grand old hymns every morning, and at the beginning of study hour in the evening. On one side the singing came from the Karen school, and on the other from the Burmese, but the songs were the same in any language. The mixture of races at the school did not always produce as much harmony as the singing. Mr. Lim, the Chinese, was more at home and certainly more at ease with his violin than with his voice. If we had an aristocrat among us, it was he—a gifted student, but never interested in after-school football or any other exercise. While the boys were bathed in mud on the playing field, he played his violin in the dormitory.

In March 1940, the Wiatts retired, and Clarence became president of the Baptist Divinity School of Burma. Clarence and I started holding English-style dinner parties for the students as part of their training. Although their future work would be in one of the many cultures of Asia, they should be at ease if circumstances found them in the company and customs of English people. I was proud of their grooming and good manners at our table. Conversation easily slipped into a variety of languages, and if the fun-loving Indian, Victor Joseph, was one of the group, he could not resist a sly remark to Pieday, our Indian serving boy. That always brought an unusual smile to Pieday's dignified air. After dinner we played games or arranged some form of entertainment. On one clear night we borrowed the college telescope to view the three moons of Jupiter.

From the ridge, hardly high enough to be called a hill, the ground sloped leisurely toward the highway. This provided a good-sized grass front which served as a playing field. The grass was no problem because our Indian neighbors kept cows, which came and went at will. We called them our "lawnmowers."

During the rains I renewed my favorite leisure pastime, and began writing again. Slowly *The Ivory Carver* took shape. When I finished writing, I put it away to simmer. A year later I shared it with a few friends to test its worth, both as literature and as a true picture of how the church in Burma grew. When I showed it to the head of the publication department of our American Baptist Mission Press in Rangoon, he suggested we publish the book. He and I began gathering ideas for an attractive paperback book. He was new to the country, however, and questioned the climax, saying he could not conceive of a Buddhist becoming a "believer" so easily. I refused to change the story, knowing my experience in Burma covered many years. I knew it was not a misrepresentation, though, admittedly, not often did Burmese come to faith in Christ quickly.

Everyone knew Hitler was preparing for war. We read his

slogan: "Guns instead of butter." Other incidents also gave advance notice. When World War II was declared on September 3, 1939, Americans as "neutrals" were not disturbed. But when the blitz of 1940 leveled London, the whole world was shocked. Clarence and I knew this war would not be as "mild" for Asia as World War I had been. We had not yet learned that modern warfare must either cease, or increase in its horrors of destruction.

The continuing war of Japan against China—by then in its eighth year—brought exiled missionaries from China to Rangoon. They told us startling personal experiences of how those who did not cooperate with the Japanese army were treated. They recounted tales of torture and the infamous "water treatment." With all its eastern seaports blockaded, China built a road over the mountains of Yunnan province to connect with an old paved road from Rangoon. That road became China's only route for military supplies from the United States, which overflowed local warehouses.

Rangoon was flooded with an influx of Chinese laborers, Chinese supervisors, and black market profiteers. Hurriedly and incompetently assembled trucks were driven to the Burmese city of Lashio near the Chinese border. From there, the Chinese laid cracked stone in muddy trails, and named it, as roads in Asia are often named, from its destination. This "Burma Road" constantly washed away and was repaired by human hands. Yet trucks, ambulances, and war material of all kinds sped over cliffs and mountains. Only a few of the convoys arrived in China. Whether the cargo was used by the Japanese, by Chiang Kai-shek's fleeing army, or by the Chinese communists, who knows?

It was inevitable that the Japanese would close this "backdoor port" of China. At least I thought so. Clarence is the sort of person who does not face trouble until it comes. I have always believed that by anticipating an emergency, I am better able to meet it. Clarence, however, felt responsible for the students at the Divinity School and had trenches dug at the back of the school and near our house. The government press issued subtle warnings, and the American Consul urged missionaries to send women and children out of the country. Judson College made plans to send students home if necessary. The public was apprehensive, but we at the Divinity School carried on our routine of classes, mindful of the fighter planes practicing overhead, but not disturbed by them. We had been sent on a mission that war would not stop.

While the bombing of Rangoon would not have surprised us, the Pearl Harbor incident on December 7, 1941, came as a complete surprise. On that infamous day, we heard the announcement of all-out war by Japan on China, England, and the United States. I understand that surprise is listed as an excellent military strategy in war manuals.

The United States was no longer neutral. Clarence and I were now potential prisoners of war. We little knew to what extent the storm winds of war would drive us across India. On December 7 we only knew that war had arrived. On the fern-bordered side verandah of our home where we drank morning coffee, I began making chalk marks on the wooden door each morning, counting the days of peace granted us by the Japanese. Many times the thought came to me: it would be just like them to spring another surprise on Christmas Day! That was a horrible thought—one I tried to put out of my mind. But my sense of being prepared impelled me to call Pieday and Anthony and the *mali* (gardener) for a talk. "From now on," I told them, "when you hear the sirens, it is not just a practice; it is the real thing." The trench offered our only safety. Preparations for Christmas went on as usual. School would be closed over New Year's but we had guests coming, and we always entertained the families of the school teachers and staff.

Clarence and I decided if conditions were such that we could not teach at the Divinity School, we would take the two senior students, Ma Sone and Keviyalay, to some hill station and give them the prescribed work of the final two months before they were to graduate. That was our plan, although we wondered if they would go. Ma Sone said to me, "I will go anywhere you go." But what if all the women were all sent away? After much discussion and prayer, Clarence and I decided to go—or to stay— together. The younger men would send their wives ahead; they could walk over the mountains to India. Remembering the Chin Hills, I knew Clarence was not physically up to that walk. So, for the present, the matter rested and we carried on as before. The chalk marks numbered ten the day Japan dropped its first bomb on Rangoon, December 23, 1941.

It was 10:30 a.m. on a beautiful clear day. The bright blue sunshine had always indicated beauty and peace. Not anymore, when men organize destruction to its ultimate horror. A friend on one of the ships in Rangoon port told of watching the planes make a straight run over the warehouses, dropping their "eggs" in perfect precision. Then they flew in low over the streets and machine-gunned thousands of people. This, too, is called good military strategy, for it "softens resistance."

Our trench had no cover, and the servants who crowded in with Clarence and me kept calling my attention to the display overhead: the burning planes falling and the fighting above us. When the siren sounded ALL CLEAR, we each went about our work, but with a new understanding of what a day might bring.

In a few hours after those first bombs fell, we noticed crowds of people on the highway heading north. All day and all night for many days that pilgrimage of stricken families seeking safety in some distant jungle village passed Seminary Hill. One person said to me, "If the British want to hold Rangoon, they may. It's not our city anyway. Why should we stay to be killed?" As the numbers on the road increased, Clarence and I realized they represented all races, all classes—some would have to walk hundreds of miles, for they were Indians fleeing to their homeland without money to hire a conveyance. A few had been able to hire a *gharry,* and in one I saw a well-fed goat with the fortunate family. The crowd was mostly laborers: longshoremen from the warehouses, servants of the rich, coolies from the city. How could any organized life continue without laborers?

On December 24 an alarm sounded, but no enemy planes got through. The next bombing came at the usual hour, 10:30 a.m. on Christmas Day. By now we had a protecting cover on our trench. Anthony was no longer entertained by skyfights, nor could I knit very well in the dark trench. Later I discovered that the number of bombs dropped actually matched the number of stitches I missed. It was 2 p.m. when we vacated the trench, and our half-cooked Christmas dinner was not Anthony's fault.

In our drawing room, I trimmed a little Christmas tree and invited the servants and their families to come at 4 p.m. This was always a highlight of the year. Each child who was old enough took part in the little program that proceeded the giving of presents. Anthony played his flute, and his children, Thomas and Zepharine, sang "Hark, The Herald Angels Sing" in their own language. Pieday's little 4-year-old Po-pah sang an Indian song with much fervor and poise.

Just before 4 p.m., a messenger called Clarence to the mission high school in the city, which had taken a direct hit and was on fire. Clarence missed the tree ceremony and, in his place, I told the Christmas story. But there were presents for all, and if you did not look at that painful procession on the road, you could forget the bombings for a brief half hour.

But even here on Seminary Hill we could not escape the results of the bombings. The *mali* dropped to his knees, put his head on my feet, and told me—in tears—that his brother had been one of the casualties in the city. He had no other relatives in Burma. I suggested that he take the next ship to India.

The students dispersed to take care of their families, getting out of the city by any possible means. Mr. Lim collected his wife and baby and headed for China via Lashio. Only one day beyond the border, they were caught in a bombing on the Burma Road. His wife and baby were both killed. Joolindra, from Thailand, made a hurried exit and got across the border just before it closed. There was no hope now of any school in Rangoon or Insein opening after New Year's Day.

Students from Nagaland had no intention of leaving Burma. Megosieso found work in Rangoon. Keviyalay did not tell us what he was going to do, but years later I heard he had secured permission from a Japanese officer to hide and save the Divinity School library. When normal living was restored after the war, the library was intact even to the original Judson Bible printed in 1840. Kevi was an excellent scholar, a lover of books. He was also a rabid Nationalist for his own people and, while in Burma, shared the national interests of the Burmese. Was he trying to prepare me for the Japanese occupation when he said, "If we must have a foreign power to govern us, we prefer it be of our own race"? For the Burmese, that meant the Japanese. Perhaps—I hate to think it—he was one of the sympathizers who, when the first bomb dropped, was heard to shout, "Our deliverers have come!" Kevi and his brother knew the Japanese shipping world, for his brother was a cargo supervisor at the Rangoon port who frankly told us that his relationship with the Japanese officers was much more pleasant than with crews of other ships.

Once we had to jump into the trench at night, hastily grabbing our shoes and coats which we kept within reach beside the bed. Anthony and his family, who lived in a little house near our back door, joined us in the trench. We spread a blanket on the earth, where the two children, Thomas and Zepharin, slept soundly. On the Sunday following Christmas, December 28, Clarence preached at Insein Baptist church. Friends at church were full of tales of the disaster in the city, but we did not linger to listen. We must reach the relative safety of our home before the dangerous hour of 10 p.m. That evening we wrote letters home, and Clarence prepared other important papers, including our wills.

On Monday morning, December 29, 1941, I made ready to sit out the war. To prepare to leave Burma was as far from my thinking as the sky itself. I moved the big teak chest to the drawing room, where it could easily be pulled out in the open if the house were bombed. In it I packed all my best linen collected through the years, my Crown Derby tea set, Clarence's silk academic gown, my charming collection of miniature marble vases, ivory carvings which Clarence had given me for special occasions, and clothing that we would need when we went home. I also filled two suitcases. Then I called the house staff and said, "We plan to stay right here and we will take care of you. We have rice and food for you if the shops close." I also made quarts of strong tea—the only remedy I knew for bad burns. I recalled one more thing—my best silver—kept in a locked drawer of the buffet. *The silver should go into the chest,* I thought, but an interruption called me away, and I never got back to the drawer.

Clarence came home for lunch from the Karen dormitory where he had been advising the few remaining students. "Evidently the planes aren't coming today," we commented to one another. I went upstairs for the usual rest period. Within minutes, I heard someone calling me. I went downstairs to find missionaries Helen Hunt and Muriel Smith looking grave. They told me they had been sent to tell the Chaneys that the mission decided it was time to send the women and children to India for safety. The husbands would stay in Burma as long as possible, then would get to India by whatever route remained open to them. They added, "The missionaries all want the Chaneys to go to Calcutta first, to receive and help the women there."

After Helen and Muriel left, I sat in stunned silence. They had used the word "invasion," which could mean concentration camp. Very well, Clarence and I could handle that. But what good could we do for anyone? Our very presence could endanger local friends. Just then, Clarence was called to the phone in a nearby house. The American Consul wanted the Chaneys to go to Calcutta on a ship leaving at 5 p.m. With a common thought, we knelt in prayer beside the cane settee. As we prayed, we received God's guidance. For the first time, we seriously considered leaving Burma.

At this point, the field secretary, the mission treasurer, and the chairman of the Reference Committee, arrived from the city to persuade us to leave. I sat in silence during their arguments. As soon as they could be ready, the women and children were to be sent to India for safety. It would greatly relieve their burdens if the Chaneys were on hand to receive and help them in that huge, bewildering city where our mission had no office. Clarence was known and loved by all the 150 missionaries of the American Baptist Mission in Burma. The three men also hinted most kindly that Clarence would be a heavy responsibility if the time came for those who were left to walk over the Himalayan foothills to Assam, India. At 3 p.m., I heard Clarence say, "Well, if I can be of more help now in Calcutta than here, I am willing to go." Then turning to me, he added, "If you will." I could not answer. I was choked with tears and went upstairs to pack. We had to leave at 4:30. I could not bear the burden of refusal when everyone else thought it right for us to leave, and the alternative placed on everyone. But my heart kept saying, "No, no! When did missionaries ever run from their posts?" Then my brain answered, "You have no post now. It is closed."

Soon everyone on Seminary Hill knew what was happening. But not Pieday, who went about setting up the tea table on the verandah as always. Fellow missionary Mr. Grady packed into a trunk whatever I gathered and threw at him. I could hardly see for tears. Papers and diaries were quickly gathered from my desk, and Mr. Grady constantly thought of things I had forgotten. Later I found many surprises in that trunk.

In the stress of the hour, no one thought of the chest of treasures "to be saved," and I never knew what became of it. While I packed, Clarence stayed at his desk. In his usual methodical care of every responsibility entrusted to him, he had closed the account books and handed them to the field secretary. He signed school reports. He called the house staff and gave them three months' advance salary. He told them to look after the house and assured them we would be back to open school in June. I could not share his optimism. Everything in our home called to me a farewell—this is the end. You will never return. Someone said, "It's 4:30—time to go."

At the foot of the stairs, I found the servants in tears and several of the neighbors gathered in stunned silence. If we could only explain; if we could only tell them why we were compelled to go because of the needs of other missionaries. But there was no time for explanations. Clarence and I rode the familiar route to Rangoon in our little Fiat.

Chapter 12

LEAVING BURMA

The American Consul and Captain Madden of the *Louise Lykes* were waiting for us at the jetty. As Mr. Grady helped me out of the car, I understood his smile of triumph and his surprise at my tears. For months he had been telling our mission that the women and children and the Chaneys should leave Burma. At last, the Chaneys were on their way; the others would follow. On the way down the river to where the ship was anchored, Captain Madden tried to divert our sadness by praising his ship. He assured us that we would enjoy the new furnishings and the good beds. But he had no praise for the city of Rangoon, which "smelled of death." Captain Madden had arrived the day after the bombings. Not only were there no labor crews to unload his cargo, there were no street cleaners to wash away the flesh of victims mowed down in the streets by machine guns.

Since he couldn't offload in Rangoon, Captain Madden appealed to Washington through the American Consul and was told to unload in Calcutta. On hearing this, Mr. Grady rushed to tell us of this rare opportunity. And here we were, just a few hours later. The *Louise Lykes* was indeed a beautiful ship on its first trip—one of the "Victory Ships," as they were called. We were seven passengers: Clarence and I, a missionary woman, and four Chinese men in charge of unloading the cargo. As we entered Calcutta, we were held a day or two at anchor on the Hooghly River. On January 3, 1942, we disembarked and presented ourselves to Dr. and Mrs. Walter Griffiths, in charge of the American Methodist Mission Guest House. This three-story building, called

Lee Memorial, was established for transient missionaries in memory of the Lee children, who were killed in a mudslide.

Clarence and I arrived late in the afternoon and announced that others from Burma would soon arrive. We were welcomed to what would be our home for two-and-a-half months while Clarence gave his time and care to the procession of evacuees from Burma, Thailand, Malaya, and China.

Clarence spent his first day in Calcutta getting necessary registration from the American Consul, from the city police, and from the Port Office, where he was given a pass to visit every ship from Rangoon. He was assured of being given a two-hour notice of each ship's arrival. On our second day in Calcutta, the stream of missionary women and children began. Clarence was on his way to learn the names and locations of different jetties when a *gharry* full of children, waving their arms and shouting to him from the street, warmed his heart. Here were two mothers and eight children in two *gharries,* hoping to see a familiar face in this foreign city. In the heat and dust, Clarence met ships, made train and hotel reservations when Lee Memorial overflowed, and helped evacuees get to the police and to their destinations, sometimes shifting plans with little notice. Many people had no plans at all. Some, learning of a mission which needed help, stayed in India for the duration of the war. By the time all entrance channels to Calcutta closed, thousands of evacuees of many races had passed through this port.

During our stay in Calcutta, Clarence and I watched Burma die. The Japanese invasion came in over the hills behind Moulmein, from Thailand, where a thousand Burmese had hidden for a year, training for this "day of deliverance." Newspapers in India repeated the lines from Burma: "The situation worsens, but Rangoon will be held." Nothing was held. One town after another fell. Thirty exiled missionaries sat at the breakfast table listening to the news. One missionary said, "Now Britain's humiliation is complete." By the end of March 1942, the Japanese military held the whole country of Burma, which remained under Japanese control for four years.

Occasionally Clarence and I considered what we should do. As long as we could be of help, we would not consider going home, although the Board announced that everyone was free to return to North America if they thought it was wise. Some who were due for furlough did go, but families waiting to be reunited hesitated to make that decision.

While in Calcutta, Clarence received urgent requests from our mission in Gauhati, Assam, asking for his help there as soon as the work in Calcutta was finished. The request from Gauhati was for student work, which appealed to Clarence, and for a pastor to take charge of an Anglo-Indian church. We agreed to go to Assam, but first Clarence needed a rest. The hill station of Darjeeling was just a night's train ride from Calcutta. Without foresight or planning, we found the winds of war carrying us to a beautiful place for an unexpected rest.

But the winds of war change like a cyclone's gale. By the time we were scheduled to go to Gauhati, war had drawn closer. The university could not open, so that ended the student work. Still, the missionary in charge in Gauhati said to come, so Clarence went alone to look the situation over while I stayed in Darjeeling. In a few days, he wired for me to come and to bring my friend Frieda along. She and I had traveled together on the ship to Burma in 1910. She had often visited us in Rangoon, and now the winds of war had blown us together in this delightful place. She had no urge to go "home," and was delighted to take up a work in Assam with us.

When we arrived in Gauhati, the British Army had already commandeered the spacious Mission compound. The army was preparing two projects: the defense of India, and the re-entry into Burma. In Calcutta, we had seen many signs of the first of the army's goals. To protect India, "the jewel in the crown" of the British Empire, Calcutta's stately buildings—the Victoria Memorial, the Government House, and the Post Office—had been painted gray. Trenches had been dug in the parks and open squares. Brick walls had been built at the entrance to stores and public buildings. Japanese planes had already visited Calcutta. The reconnaissance planes had come over the city, too high to be gunned from below, and then too low—barely above the tree tops—to be gunned down. Would this war follow us everywhere? Now we were in Assam, even nearer to the point of Japanese invasion.

The American Baptist Mission compound in Gauhati lay along the bank of the great Bhramaputra River. The compound consisted of bamboo *bashas* (houses) with the exception of the chapel at one end and the home of the missionary in charge at the other end. The compound had now become Rest Camp No. 6 for the British Army, where 1,500 BOR's (British Other Ranks, similar to American GI's) could spread themselves on the bamboo floors for a few hours or a few days of rest on their way to and from the Burma front. The troops, Wingate's Maurauders, passed through Gauhati and went on. Many did not return. Frieda and I asked no questions and received no information. We were there only to serve the soldiers, who, we noticed, were not young boys, but largely men who left families in danger at home.

The one empty building on the mission compound was a student hostel with no students to fill it. We turned the lower floor into a reading room with tables and whatever literature we could scrounge for the soldiers. It became known as the Mission Canteen at Gauhati, and was popular with the soldiers. The room boasted an organ and a record player. To the strains of the men's favorite song, *"Over the Rainbow"* (played over and over), Frieda and I and local missionary women served eggs and chips, buttered bread, and tea by the gallon. The men insisted on paying for everything they ate, so Frieda and I set prices as low as we could, since we hated charging them at all.

To protect the Assam Railway, which ran through Gauhati,

gun sites were established on both sides of town. At the small ack-ack gun sites, a crew of 30 men kept watch day and night. A Welsh company of 140 men lived at an artillery gun called Big Bertha. This Gauhati area for changing troops had no army chaplain. Hearing that a missionary from Burma lived nearby, the Commander asked Clarence to organize religious services for the men. Clarence was glad to do so, on condition that he receive no pay from the military. We wanted no part of this war, which was no longer a fight between soldiers, but an organized destruction of civilian life and property.

Clarence established a program of several services each week. Once a week, he and I rode to the duck pond and held a service for the few men on ack-ack gun duty. On another day, we gathered in the open near the big guns for a service. Transport was provided by the military, so I was once again climbing ladders. This time they weren't rope ladders over the sides of ships, but iron ladders to the high seat of a gun carriage when that was the only military conveyance available. The folding organ and I accompanied the temporary chaplain wherever he went. Clarence also conducted a Sunday night service at the Mission chapel.

Every Tuesday and Thursday night, Clarence held a ten-minute religious service at the Canteen for the transients in the compound. Clarence printed a statement that allowed men to leave, stay, or join in at their leisure. Few soldiers left, and most expressed gratitude for the help the service provided. More than one man, as he stacked his rifle inside the door, said he never missed this night if he could help it. That ten minutes was packed with singing a hymn, reading verses of Scripture, and offering a prayer full of understanding of the anxieties these men carried, a plea to God for their families and for the presence of God in their lives. Then the chatter and clatter of games and dishes began again. Clarence sat at the tables with the men, learning much of their backgrounds. "The Old Rugged Cross" became the favorite hymn, even for the Jewish boys. We heard that the soldiers sang it in their lorries as they traveled.

We also visited hospitals. I spent three hours a day in the most pitiful of all, the evacuee hospital. It was a wretched building where the sick and dying remnant of the overland trek that had begun in Burma that day of December 23, 1941, ended up. These were the few—the very few— left from among the thousands who had walked that "Via Dolorosa" over impossible jungle trails and mountains. Friends, parents, and children had been left beside the trail while these few managed to take a few more steps and arrive at the railhead. Having reached India, they were removed from trains and boats, wasted and exhausted from famine, unable to tell their names. They at least had a dry, covered place in which to die, though they slept on pallets of straw on a cement floor. There was no nursing staff, no doctors—only sporadic volunteer care from local hospitals.

Clarence visited the military hospital and the men housed in a ward borrowed from our American Baptist Mission hospital. There he made many lasting friendships. Post-war letters from some of these men told of a new view of the value of missions and of the Christian witness they now experienced. Many of those men gave their lives to Christian service in England. Italian nuns who wanted information about bombing staffed the civil hospital, always overflowing with patients. When the ward filled up, they asked me, "What shall we do?" I suggested the only thing possible, "Put the patients under the beds." At first the sisters all laughed. None of them could believe I was serious until it happened.

The BOR's had spurned the trench beside the Mission Canteen until a junior officer walked into the room shouting, "Gentleman, to the trench!" Once there, they had to endure the jeers from civilians passing by who laughed to see the British army sitting in a grave-like, earthen trench. I happened to be at the post office when the first ALERT was sounded. One man and I sat in the trench while a boy on a bicycle began shouting,

"Our deliverers have come!" No bombs were dropped that day, nor on any day while Clarence and I were in Gauhati, but when we passed through Calcutta later, we saw that city had not escaped destruction.

Clarence spent less than a full year at Gauhati, yet his deep devotional messages were long remembered by the men of the British Army in those tragic days. His Christian faith and witness helped people of many classes. After Clarence's death in 1969, a retired captain of the Irrawaddy Flotilla Company wrote to me, "I address this to Clarence as well as to you, as he is one of those rare spirits whom one cannot accept as having passed away, for he achieved immortality not only in another world, but in the minds of the many people in many lands who were privileged to know his friendship. So long as they live, he, too, lives on."

From June of 1942 to March of 1943, we carried a full daily schedule of various duties. Clarence was beginning to show the strain, not only from the work, but also the wearing uncertainties of the time. We received no good word from Burma; in fact, no word at all. Our night's rest was often broken by the steady march of hundreds on the street. When the steps faltered at our gate, we knew that in the morning we would see the *bashas* full of weary men who would flood the Canteen asking for more duck eggs than we could get. Clarence needed a rest, and when the Board called for a conference of all "Burma missionaries living in India" to be held in April, he said we should go. Frieda decided to stay on at the Canteen. The thought of seeing our co-workers brought joyous anticipation, but it meant a train ride of over 1,000 miles across northern India. The conference was to meet in Mussoorie, the hill station above Dehra Dun.

The map of India is a great triangle, with Assam at the upper right point and Kashmir at the left upper point, more than 2,000 miles apart. When Clarence and I left Gauhati, we knew we would not return. Clarence could never again carry a full schedule of preaching or mission work. Perhaps it was time for us to return home. A British doctor had said that sooner or later, Clarence must have an operation, and we "should go home for it." But this was no time to travel the seas. Clarence and I discussed it again and again before dropping the subject. God would show us our next step. A change would be good for us both, and we turned our faces to the conference, saddened by the thought that we were moving farther and farther from Burma.

After a long day and night on the dusty train, a short bus ride from the Dehra Dun station took us 6,000 feet up to the houses and schools perched one above the other on the hillsides of Mussoorie. Here was the American School, well staffed and competent to prepare American children for college or university in the United States. The majority of students were missionary children. The great Himalayan range, the bulwark of India, was still our skyline, but the peaks were not as high as those we had seen from Darjeeling. Yet they hovered over us in protecting care and majestic beauty.

The conference provided a great reunion. A few of the Burma missionaries working in India could not attend because of work or health, or because distances in India are vast. But 35 of us assembled in this lovely spot, tied by links of pre-war service in the land we loved. The joy of seeing these friends again and the lift of spirit Clarence and I gained revived us and made the long, tiresome journey worthwhile. The war seemed far away. We could almost think it didn't exist, until the conference agenda took up the business of making plans to return. Did these missionaries not know, as we did, the tremendous uncertainties of even the military plans for "the big push" back into Burma? "Going back" was a tangle of complications—the Ledo Road to be built over a jungle trail strewn with whitening skeletons; even the possibility of further Japanese invasion of India, which did take place a year later.

Yet most of the considerations and plans of the conference had to do with "the return"—to anticipate the needs and wise policies for a people and a church deprived of its leaders, of property, of homes, but not of its Christian faith and witness. Of that we were sure. And our faith in the Burmese Christians was not misplaced. As one who returned after the war said, "They had endured the fiery furnace like the Hebrew children, and like them, there was not even the smell of smoke upon them." There had been added to their testimony the experience of the presence of the living Christ in the midst of their hardship. "Now we *know*," they said. "Before we endured suffering, we only believed in our heads. But during the war, Christ was with us all the time."

When the conference convened, Clarence was asked to be the chairman. He declined and asked to be relieved from all committee work. I think they could see he really was not well enough to serve them as he used to. We had a doctor among us, and during a check-up, Clarence had shown such a debilitated condition that the doctor ordered "Three months' complete rest with *no* work." Several jobs were suggested for Clarence "after the rest," but the one for which his long service best qualified him was a complete report of all property of the American Baptist Mission left in Burma at the time of evacuation, including land, buildings, and equipment. This was to be done "as soon as he feels like it," the conference said. Clarence had visited every American Baptist Mission station and he knew every one of the staff, whether in India or in the United States. He could take time preparing his report.

After the summer's rest, if Dr. Chaney felt equal to undertake this task, a place would be provided at Lahore where he could work in cooperation with the Mission treasurer, D. O. Smith. Forman Christian College (Presbyterian) had given the Burma Mission-in-Exile a residence and an office there. The question plaguing Clarence and me had been answered. We were not to return to America; we still had opportunity to serve.

Since we were not to go home yet, where would we go for

this prescribed rest? There was no place in Mussoorie, with every apartment and guest room spoken for by emergencies connected with war in China, in Burma, and everywhere else arising daily. Kashmir was not far away. We were advised to go there, and were offered the provision of a tent and full board. Dr. S. Sheets conducted groups of tenters who went to Pahlgam each summer. Without ever having such a plan in mind, now we were given a summer in Kashmir! How could we explain such perfect favors of loving care from a heavenly Father? How the past months fitted into a picture and pattern that had supplied every need and rare blessings unaccounted for by human planning. We could look back over all the experiences since January 1942 and find that each step had been prepared for us.

Taking the train from Dehra Dun, Clarence and I stopped for a day at Lahore to see the place where we would live beginning in September. We spent another day at Ralwaldpindi to see missionary co-workers, the Jurys, who were settled there for the duration of the war, working in a mission college. In this traditionally romantic corner of India we were among names that I knew from poetry and song: Srinagar, Amritsar, Lahore, Rawalpindi, and the Khyber Pass. Songs such as "Pale hands I loved beside the Shalimar," and "Less than the dust." From 'Pindi we traveled to Srinagar, a ride through wild country with snow-capped peaks always in sight. We were familiar with the eastern end of the Himalayas where we saw Mt. Everest and the peaks of the Kanchenjunga from Darjeeling. Now at the western end, we saw a group of towering giants 20,000–30,000 feet high: Annapurna, K2, Nanga Parbat, and others well known to mountain climbers.

Our rough road led through tremendous boulders and rocks, but all along the way we viewed surprising beauty. Here and there stood wild oleanders, wild roses, pines, *deodars,* buttercups, *chanar* trees, and, at last, down from the wild crags into the Vale of Kashmir, where long lines of poplars bordered the river of Abana right into the little city of Srinagar.

The motels of Srinagar are not buildings, but boats. Long, wide, and flat-bottomed, they anchor in a canal to the lake where tame hoopoe birds feed on the bank. Pahlgam was our destination, but we had to wait until Dr. Sheets finished his work at Forman College and set up his tent home for the summer. The day after we arrived was Clarence's 65th birthday, June 5, 1943. I was able to buy a birthday cake, and two Rangoon missionary friends joined us for the party. The front compartment of the houseboat (named *Pompa Dour*) had ample room for all of us.

The next day, the reaction and let-down from the constant arduous work of the past 15 months in the heat of Assam and the lack of normal living, combined with that 65th birthday, which every missionary man dreaded, made it necessary to call a doctor. Clarence lay in bed for a few days. To be officially "retired" was bad enough, but to be ordered to three months without work was a heavy drag. Since the age of 13, Clarence had never known life without work. It had been constant, year after year— to earn money, to study, to finance his schooling, to give himself and all his time to the work of the mission to which he was assigned. Now he was weak, facing three months of "idleness," as he put it. It had always been the Board's policy if, at the age of retirement, a missionary wanted to work on and if the Reference Committee advised it, he could do so with an annual assignment. I could see that now my mission was to help Clarence regain physical and spiritual strength with the objective of returning to service. To make the rest effective for the task awaiting him was our new responsibility.

Srinagar is a lovely city of trees, lakes, canals, birds, and the attractive Kashmiri people—the most handsome race I have ever seen. Clarence and I enjoyed Dahl Lake, the Shalimar Gardens, and *shakari* rides under the full moon. We also learned in various ways that we still lived in the British Empire, though who controlled Kashmir was a puzzle. It was Prime Minister Nehru's ancestral home and Hindu in its laws, which prohibited eating beef. A tin of "bully beef" carried in our bags for "emergency food" had inadvertently not been declared at the border customs. When Dr. Sheets heard about this, it became an embarrassment to us all. Eventually we buried it deep in Kashmiri soil.

One day at the post office, I stood in a long line at the stamp window. The day when a white face would have quickly been spotted and asked to the head of the line was a thing of the past. It was only as I neared the window that I discovered in the line ahead of me a stark naked Hindu holy man. However, his body was liberally covered with ashes, which explained why I had not noticed him sooner.

On June 18th we moved on by crowded bus to Pahlgam, as paying guests of Dr. Sheets in his summer home of tents at 7,000 feet altitude. The big tent served as the dining room. We enjoyed the 9 p.m. dinner and coffee by a fireplace inside the tent. The nights were very cold; we went to our *charpoy*-cot beds in warm pajamas, bed socks, sweaters, and bathrobes, with hot water bottles and heated stones at our feet. The whole valley was dotted with tents. At one time we heard there were 1,100 people, mostly Indians, on vacation. The days were sunny, beautiful, and long. It was hardly dark at bedtime. Through the whole valley was heard the song of the turbulent Lidder River. When the season's logs began coming down from the mountains, Clarence and I spent an afternoon watching two men with long poles and hooks working the log jam. The bright sun, the whirling water, the roar—perhaps I wasn't too strong myself—anyway, I fainted, and Clarence had to walk to the village for help. He brought back coolies and a dolly on which they carried me to our tent. I was kept in bed for two days.

Another visit to the bazaar section of town was more successful. It was our wedding anniversary and, as usual, Clarence insisted we must buy a present. I scorned the idea of finding anything in this place that we would want. But we would try. Two shops dealt largely in onions, nails, flour, and tools. But local men who do the beautiful Kashmiri embroidery seen on the Nand rugs sometimes leave a bit of their handiwork in a friend's shop for sale. And so it was, as we lingered in a truly primitive atmosphere, I found a tea cozy of goat hair embroidered in lovely rose-colored flowers. Tea cozies have always been my delight, and I could never make tea without one. So I decided that the only thing I wanted was that tea cozy. The price was 8 *annas*—26 cents at the time. Clarence spurned such a gift for our special day. It was nothing; it didn't cost enough. But I insisted I wanted nothing else. It became the pride and joy of my tea table after retirement, though when I returned to our tent I did not find it so comforting, for it reminded me that I was an evacuee with no home, no tea table, and no teapot. What did I want with a tea cozy? I loved it because Clarence had wanted us to have a special remembrance of our anniversary, and it traveled with me all the rest of our days by land and sea—a promise, I thought, of a home somewhere, someday.

Clarence and I spent our days in the open. I planned walks and picnics. A local man, Shabana, helped us build a fire and roast potatoes. We could picnic anywhere we wished. There was no work as such, just reading, writing letters, and long hours of rest. But it did not build Clarence up as I had hoped. He was far removed from mission concerns in Burma; he was not serving on any mission committee. Clarence could not accept retirement. He began to feel that he could serve Burma better on deputation work at home than out here, and he did not see much value in the task that awaited him at Lahore. He was definitely wrong on that score.

There was no adequate medical care available at Pahlgam, and although his organic disorder had not worsened, Clarence could not forget the possibility of an imminent medical emergency. He was thin and an ash-gray color. With much prayer and thought we carried through the uncertain days till September and then took the bus to Lahore. I felt sure that once there, he would relish the work that only he could do.

Forman Christian College, one of the oldest in northwest India, had recently moved out of the crowded old city into a beautiful, spacious new campus. All the new buildings were built of white cement. The residences for faculty members, whether foreign missionaries or nationals, were simple in design but spacious. In one of the empty bedrooms was the office of the Burma Mission-in-Exile where D.O. and Clarence worked. It was wonderful to see Clarence smiling and happy again, intent for four hours a day on records collected from memory and from endless correspondence to missionaries in the United States and in India. Once more he felt needed in the mission work to which he had given his life. And it was work of value after all. Years later, at the memorial service held for him, particular mention was made of Clarence's last task: "The Society records its gratitude that Dr. Chaney so carefully preserved the complete record of its property in Burma, bringing it to the U.S.A. on his return in 1944."

We were again among young people. The college enrollment was 1,100, of which only eleven were girls. Brave girls, lovely in their *saris* and serious about their education. We had no contact with the classes, but saw abundant proof that the school was a man's world, for the boys were everywhere, in the conventional dress of the Punjab. When dressed up in their long white coats and butterfly turbans, they looked like men. When we saw them drying their long, curly hair in the sun after a shampoo, they did not belong to any conventional pattern we knew except for the conspicuous textbooks in their hands. Time for study must not be wasted. They were schoolboys, after all.

In the late afternoon, Clarence and I could again share the companionship of long walks. A favorite one was the walk into town. Lahore is the city Kipling writes about: an old city of impressive buildings. It was a delightful walk of four miles, and after tea in town we could ride home on the college bus. The first time we saw the Zam Zam cannon in front of the "wonder house," there were six little Kims playing on and around it. The canal which bordered one side of the campus interested us. When it was full for irrigation purposes, we walked down to the big waterwheel, where a ragged, disgruntled-looking camel walked round and round, hour after hour, occasionally encouraged by a small boy and a stick. By this simple method, water was lifted in the wooden buckets that rimmed the wheel and emptied themselves into irrigation ditches for the fields. The canal was a favorite walking place anytime, but especially when a full moon showed through the lace canopy of eucalyptus trees on the bank.

The Mission treasurer's wife, Muriel, and I found many ways to serve the community. Lahore had been named by the military as a suitable place for BOR's and GI's to spend their two weeks of rest. Our home was open to them anytime, and we offered to put two of them up for the full two weeks. The American boys preferred to stay in the city. But two of the British boys came for the two weeks and wanted nothing more entertaining than the quiet of a home. They were in the Air Force and had just arrived from duty over Burma. They could name for us the familiar spots where bombs were dropped. The conversation was painful to us, but we wanted any information of that land we could get.

Much was being done for the British and American soldiers, but we wondered if anything was being done for the 500 Chinese soldiers being trained as pilots in a camp not far away. Their big yellow planes nearly frightened us to death when they practiced the "falling leaf" and other stunts over the college campus. Muriel and I decided we would give teas in our home for these men. When we communicated with the Commander (who was a Christian and spoke English), he responded with gratitude and said he would send ten men each time. To our dismay, the ten were all officers, only one able to communicate haltingly. Each week ten Chinese men came to our house. After tea, we played games on the lawn, and when it came time to leave, we gathered in a circle for Clarence to pray for them and their families.

Hearing that there was a tent hospital up the line where our Burmese nurses were at work, Muriel and I decided to visit them for a weekend. It was indeed a group of tents set in a muddy field far away from any habitation. In these tents lay sick Indian soldiers lying on *charpoys* with a little charcoal stove beside each bed, for it was winter and very cold. Here were our lovely nurses from Burma—Karens, Shans, and Burmese—wearing high mud boots to wade through the snow and mud, attending these Indian men of the British Army.

Major Ba Aye was in charge of the camp, and in his nicely warmed tent, Muriel and I had tea. He was shocked beyond telling to hear we had traveled in a third-class carriage, and insisted on giving us money for the return, saying that he, a Christian, knowing what we missionaries had done for his people, was humiliated that we should appear of a lower class than the "godless British Army who travel first class." To show their gratitude for our thought of them in this "forsaken corner" of the Empire, Major Ba Aye loaded us with gifts of fruit, cheese, and a live chicken which we had to take home, though the only compartment we could get was in third class with 16 other occupants.

Fewer than 50 in the Forman College student body were Christians, yet we had a Christmas play with shepherds—and Muriel as the angel Gabriel. Clarence made a magnificent wise man. I played the organ for carols, and D.O. was emcee. Attendance was good. We invited six Burma evacuees, three Anglo-Indians, and three Indians whom we had known in positions of responsibility at the Mission Press in Rangoon, to share Christmas dinner. We held a New Year's party in our home for a few missionaries and some of the Indian staff, 23 in all. After games, we served doughnuts and coffee, and just before midnight Clarence led a short prayer service. We entered the year of 1944 with prayer and praise for all God's mercies we received.

Chapter 13

TRAVELING HOME

As of March 1944, the war had not ended. Britain's "Big Push" back into Burma that Clarence and I heard so much about in Assam had not happened. In fact, it had gone the other way, and the Japanese Army actually started to invade India. The Japanese were turned back at the edge of Manipur by a frightening sacrifice of British soldiers. There was no promise of a soon return to Burma for civilians, least of all for us seniors. Clarence and I had now completed 35 years of missionary service (only 34 for me), and our last furlough had been five years ago. Clarence finished a fair-sized book of reports and inventories for the Board. His operation was also pending. It was time to go home where we could still help the church in Burma. Of course the sea was not "safe." Where was anyone safe in a world of madness called war? Returned troop ships would carry a few passengers who wished to take the risk. Clarence and I booked on such a ship sailing from Bombay in April.

Preliminary preparations for sailing in war time made it necessary for us to arrive in Bombay early. All papers, journals, and written materials such as maps must be handed to the censor to be carefully examined. Passports and health certificates had to be in order. There was no set sailing date, but we were told "reservations have been made for your sailing. Notice will be given." While waiting, we went to Poona for a Good Friday service with Christians there. Our last Easter Sunday in India was spent in the American Methodist church, where Clarence preached at the pastor's request. After another wait, we received the telegram:

"Appear at the Ballard jetty in Bombay at 8 a.m. on April 13, 1944."

We were to set sail on a large U.S. Navy ship. I was given a berth with six other women; Clarence bunked in a cabin with six other men. This was going to be an experiment in good manners and good will to all men (and women). We were given careful instructions, assigned to the same lifeboat (thanks to the Navy for that), and must appear for boat drill twice daily "with life jacket properly fastened." Life jackets must be carried at all times. Chairs were provided at meals in the dining room but nowhere else. On the deck you either walked or sat on the floor in the little space between life rafts and other equipment. We could never forget that the sea was not safe. There was complete blackout at night. If any of us passengers braved the dark and found our way to the rail, there was great consolation in the familiar stars, the beauty of the Southern Cross, and the glory of Canopus. Our old friends were still there in the sky. And our God was still there: we were in His care.

Our ship had overhead escort for a few days out of Bombay and at each port we entered, which were few. We passengers were not allowed to leave the ship at any time, although we sat in harbor at Melbourne, Australia, for two days while 1,500 Italian prisoners-of-war were sent to help the farmers and ranchers. These, I supposed, were from the little city of 15,000 prisoners held at Dehra Dun. From the hilltop of Mussoorie we had seen the lights of that camp far away. When I asked about the camp, one of the British officers in charge there answered in a casual way, "Oh, I think they are comfortable, but the Germans are sullen and the Italians spend a lot of time weeping." As we watched the long line of men leave our ship, I noticed that about every tenth man had a crude, homemade guitar in his luggage. I was pleased to know they would sing their home songs in a strange land.

We could only guess our direction by watching the sunrise and sunset, for we zigzagged our course every five minutes of the voyage for 42 days. Suddenly we found ourselves in the Panama Canal. Then began the guessing game of ports to the north. Navy sailors darkened our cabin at sunset and opened it at sunrise when we seven women were washing and getting dressed in the one-and-a-half hours while water was turned on. We bombarded the sailors with questions. Hearing their last trip had landed them in San Francisco, we were hardly prepared for the emergency invasion of France, which took our ship to the port of Boston.

The landing on May 23, 1944, was an historic event. Not only was Boston to be our last entry, it also had been our first port of sailing. Clarence had visited Boston once since he sailed out in 1909, but I never had. After all these years, we had come home. There was a sad finality about landing (never again to see Burma?), yet a note of joy for me that never again would I have to sail the sea. From dangers known and unknown, we had been spared for retirement. Of the many dangers—excepting the one at Maubin when another step in the dark would have placed my foot atop a huge, deadly krait coiled on the path—the most calamitous of all was the explosion of an American ship in the harbor of Bombay the day after we sailed. The ship was loaded with dynamite when it caught fire. Fifteen ships in the docks sank and seven fire engines and crews disappeared. A large section of the sea front was destroyed. Yet Clarence and I sailed out to the open sea unharmed. Why were we so blessed?

I have never been able to answer the question, *Why?* when it relates to God's plan. The why of blessing is just as puzzling as the why of adversity. As I look over my life, I see a succession of blessings. When there has been adversity—frustration, disappointment, seeming calamity—the long look shows a perfect fulfillment of the promise that "all things work together for good to those who love the Lord."

Eventually Clarence and I retired in California. First in Santa Barbara to be near our old friends the W. E. Wiatts, where we spent seven happy years. Our final retirement home was in Pilgrim Place in Claremont, California, where we joined a community of 300 retired Christian workers of several denominations, who had served at home and overseas.

When age and failing strength raised the problem of caring for a home and a garden, we took an apartment in "the Lodge," where housekeeping duties were provided. Even then, Clarence's failing memory and his weakness from strokes limited our activities but not our companionship. With a walker, he still enjoyed the outdoors and our walks in park-like Pilgrim Place, and even to town. I was constantly reminded of his unfailing care for me. Never did he neglect to plan for our inevitable parting, and so often was it discussed (and forgotten) that when it came, I found every detail in order. Not with any less care and thought, but with real enthusiasm, he spoke of "the bright future" of which he was sure and at ease as he contemplated that last revelation of "the excellency of Christ Jesus." He had known and proclaimed it all his life, and Clarence will be no stranger to the presence of God.

Another stroke following a case of shingles made it necessary for Clarence to become a patient in Pilgrim Place's Rest Home. Only a driveway separated the Rest Home from the Lodge. I spent most of each day with him. As he grew weaker, he lost all interest in our world and, without any pain, he quietly slipped away to his heavenly home on September 7, 1969.

In my room at the Lodge, where Clarence shared the apartment for over six years, I live with the precious memories of our 54 years together. I know this is the place he most wanted us to live when either of us was left alone. Many friends are near and as long as God gives me these added years, I seek to fulfill whatever mission He has for me to do. Clarence and I were both the last surviving members of our families. My several nephews and two nieces live far away. Now that Clarence has been called home, I realize the peculiar type of loneliness of a person who has no one with whom to share common memories. If I occasionally feel a touch of self-pity, I remind myself of the vow of renunciation of family I made when I became a missionary in 1910, and realize with deep gratitude that only now is that vow fulfilled.

Our years in Burma spanned the "golden years of foreign missions." The 100 years of missions before we arrived were years devoted to preaching and teaching the Christian way of life, and the wise policies of those early years came to fruition in hundreds of highly trained Christian leaders who today carry on a Christian witness in well-organized churches.

Independent Burma, like an adolescent child who likes to "do it myself," has chosen to exclude all outside influence and seeks to build its new structure in rigid isolationism. Foreign missionaries are excluded from Burma today. But the church exists to preach and to teach. Evangelists walk the mountains and river valleys, telling the Good News of God's love for man. Bible schools are full of Burmese eager to share in the work of the gospel. Our 35 years in Burma were only a small part of the history of one of Asia's outstanding examples of foreign missions.

In 1830 there had been set before the missionaries the ideal of planting in Burma a self-supporting, self-governing, and self-propagating church, something that would remain if (or when) foreign missionaries should be removed. It came so suddenly that at the moment, Clarence and I were stunned. We wept and grieved—not for ourselves, but for our Christian friends. I rejoice in the letters I receive from Burma. Not in the letters alone, though they are full of love and affection, but because each one is a personal testimony of radiant Christian faith. Hard days may lie ahead, as they did during the war (for the church of

Burma has its martyrs, too), but it is God's church, and "the gates
of hell shall not prevail against it." Martin Luther expressed this
confidence well in his hymn "A Mighty Fortress is Our God."
Ostergaard, the Dutch Christian, has left it to us in another hymn:

> *That course can neither be lost nor stayed,*
> *Which takes the course which God has made,*
> *And is not trusting in walls or towers,*
> *But slowly growing from seeds to flowers.*

I have always loved the hymn "Lead Me Gently Home,
Father." When I heard the rich bass voices at Seminary Hill sing
it, "home" was an ideal of both life and death, and the rich harmony never failed to touch me to tears. How many hundreds
of those Moody and Sankey hymns have I heard sung in bamboo chapels, in high-ceilinged classrooms, in city churches of
Burma! How many miles of pedal work have my feet traveled as
we sang them in jungle churches where the folding organ always
began the services with a beautiful melody. But when the congregation sitting on the floor broke into a Sankey hymn, the harmony and enthusiasm lifted a person off his feet—except for
mine pedaling against the sagging elastic cords! Even today, I hear
most often the deep bass voices of the Karens singing, *Lead me
Gently Home* . . . and I want no better ending to the years ahead
of me than that.

Above:
Faith Baptist Bible College

Left:
Dr. S. N. Mang, president, with his family

Below:
Student body at Faith Baptist Bible College, Tiddim, northwest Myanmar

FAITH BAPTIST BIBLE COLLEGE & SEMINARY
NOVEMBER 23, 1999

Studying God's Word

Providing Christian literature

Reaching out to families and children

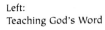

Above:
Jesus said, "Let the little children come to me."

Left:
Teaching God's Word

GLOBAL ACCESS PARTNERSHIPS

George and Debra Collins

Partnering with
Nationals

Today's "Bible Woman"

GLOBAL ACCESS
PARTNERSHIPS

A Brief History

George and Debra Collins worked with ABWE in Bangladesh from 1981 to 1993, focusing on evangelism, leadership training, and church development in the restricted hill tracts area which borders India and Burma.

During this time, they realized that the best—and sometimes the only—way to sustain work in restricted access areas was through training and sending national leaders into the otherwise unreachable towns and villages. Through the efforts of North American missionaries working among the tribes of Bangladesh, more than 100 village churches were established. A national evangelist started *every* one of those churches.

George Collins visited Burma in 1990 and learned of incredible needs and opportunities in this land where foreign missionaries were expelled in the 1960s. Someone was needed to "stand in the gap" on behalf of Burmese believers and other Christians who live in difficult places. This could be accomplished by presenting their needs to North American churches and individuals, for partnership opportunities.

In early 1993, George approached Wendell W. Kempton, then ABWE's president, and mission administrators about creating a department within ABWE to provide support for national ministries and workers around the world. The primary focus would be on partnerships in an area known as the 10/40 Window, where most of the restricted access nations of the world are located.

After researching and assessing both the need for partnerships and the desire of North Americans to support such an endeavor, George presented the program to the ABWE Board in April 1994. The ABWE Board approved the concept, accepted the proposal, and assigned George Collins to serve as its international director.

From its inception, Global Access Partnerships has been called GAP. The name indicates this ministry stands in the GAP both historically and practically. With the number of restricted access nations, coupled with the rise of the missionary work force from non-Western countries, North American mission agencies need to adjust their methods in order to spread the gospel.

Practically, it is clear that strategic partnerships with godly and like-minded friends are not an option but an increasing necessity.

New personnel join the GAP team regularly, and new partnerships with national ministries arise each year. GAP also works with ABWE's regional administrators and field teams to establish new outreaches and to assist in supporting national-led organizations in countries open to traditional missions.

Missions-minded churches in North America have always been interested in spreading the gospel into unreached areas. They were limited, however, to supporting traditional missionaries in open countries or to supporting national outreach in closed countries through organizations which did not share their same beliefs. When GAP was born, donors could have an impact on unreached areas through ABWE, an organization with which they are familiar.

GAP Involvement in Myanmar (formerly Burma)

In the early 1800s Adoniram Judson, the first American Baptist missionary, carried the gospel to the land of Burma. Since that time, many have come to Christ from the various tribal groups resident in the lush forested lands bordering India, China, and Thailand.

In 1966 Western missionaries were forced to leave the predominantly Buddhist nation. During the following three decades, the church continued its steady growth as godly national leaders maintained missionary zeal. Much remains to be accomplished, however, as many villages have yet to be reached with the gospel message. In addition, the majority Burmese population, made up of nearly 30 million Buddhists, has been resistant to Christianity since the days before Judson.

Global Access Partnerships developed a partnership which allows GAP to assist the Evangelical Baptist Churches of Burma. This fellowship of nearly 100 churches among the Chin peoples of southeastern Burma has demonstrated its faithfulness and commitment to Christ throughout the years. The Faith Baptist Bible College and Seminary, located in Chin State, has an enrollment of over 200 students. It is the largest Bible training institution in the entire nation.

The founder and president, a capable leader, has been used of God to provide essential training to hundreds of eager students. In addition to offering a Bible education, the schools are eager to mobilize teams of national missionaries to reach into areas still untouched with the gospel message.

Churches and individuals in this desperately poor nation do what they can with their meager resources. GAP helps by providing scholarship funds for eligible students who might not otherwise be able to attend the college and seminary.

In addition to scholarship funds and other expenses related

to the schools, GAP helps in evangelism efforts through projects such as providing office equipment (copiers, typewriters, office supplies) and bicycles for use by evangelists and pastors.

Why Support Nationals?

Many good reasons exist for pursuing ministry in restricted access areas by training, supporting, and encouraging national Christian leaders.

- *Language acquisition:* In certain restricted areas, it is not unusual for several language groups to be represented in close surroundings. Those native-born to such a place must, of necessity, be able to converse in numerous languages. The obvious benefit is that the gospel can be communicated immediately and most effectively by individuals indigenous to a targeted culture.

- *Cultural adaptation:* Knowing and adjusting to the cultural norms of any society takes a great deal of research, time, and commitment in order to become well versed in what is acceptable in that context. National Christians have learned from birth the acceptable standards of the culture and can minister without fear of becoming an obstacle to the message of Christ.

- *Locale accessibility:* With a growing list of countries off-limits to foreign missionaries, organizations focused on reaching into such places are devising a variety of creative outreaches. Though these may have an effect, there is no substitute for having direct access to the individuals in need. This is done most effectively through nationals who live in or near the host culture.

- *Ministry accountability:* Much is being done today in the name of Christ by both the sincere and the unscrupulous. Those who have an intimate knowledge of the area in question are the best source of accountability.

A two-fold advantage of partnering with trusted national leaders is that they can share information and insight regarding potential partners and can provide sound teaching to those who live and work in restricted access areas. This is a benefit to both sides of the partnership arrangement, as churches in North America know better how to pray and whom to support, and the national believer is better equipped to discern truth from error.

Six Steps For a Balanced Approach to Overseas Missions

These questions are often raised when discussing overseas missions: "Should we continue to send Western missionaries overseas? Isn't it cheaper to send money to support national workers?" Forty pastors attending ABWE's Pastors' Consultation on World Evangelism in March 2000 addressed this issue and concluded that balance is the key. It is not an either/or proposition. Continue to send missionaries from churches in North America *and* sponsor godly men, women, and projects in other parts of the world. The Great Commission has not been rescinded. Our Lord still says, "Go ye" to *all* believers in Christ. Perhaps the most telling statement came from Scott Forbes, former missionary to Zambia, now a missions professor: "If we only give money to support nationals, how will our children see a model of something they can become?"

Consider the following balanced approach:

1. *Send North American Missionaries*
   Career missionaries are needed in all countries where missionaries are allowed to enter. Many Restricted Access Nations also need full-time workers who combine professional skills with a gospel outreach.

2. *Seek Short-Term Opportunities*
   With the world so much more accessible than in former years, it is quite possible for people to visit a mission

field. Statistics show a high percentage of those who go into full-time missionary service already have cross-cultural experience. Short-term ministries (from two weeks to two months) provide a firsthand look at missions. Short-term possibilities vary, but the conclusion is usually the same: "We've never been the same since we went to _____."

3. *Support National Ministries*
Share in the joy of partnering with God's people who serve in difficult places. The GAP program identifies and develops relationships with groups and individuals leading outreach and discipleship efforts in over 20 countries, and assists North American churches in partnering with them.

4. *Sponsor National Missionaries*
Foreign missionaries are not allowed to serve in more than 60 countries, yet it is possible to sponsor individuals who are missionaries to their own (or a neighboring) country. These local people often face extreme conditions as they seek to impact their world for Christ.

5. *Supply Ministry Needs*
Just as churches and outreaches in North America need materials, supplies, and office equipment to operate their day-to-day activities, missionaries and nationals in other countries also need supplies for their ongoing work.

6. *Supplement Special Projects*
As ministries expand, especially in poverty-stricken areas of the world, special opportunities arise to provide funds for a building, vehicle, or large piece of equipment that are beyond the ability of believers in these places to fully finance.

For further information about GAP,
contact George Collins.

E-mail: GAPartners@aol.com